MW01601274

How to Save Your Marriage When Trust Is Broken

Discover 10 Simple Steps to Turn Your Broken Trust Into a Happy Marriage

Kate Homily

How to Save Your Marriage When Trust Is Broken - Discover 10 Simple Steps to Turn Your Broken Trust into A Happy Marriage is another project. is my third project. If you want to know more, click on the respective title, you will be reindexed pages. Your review is welcome on Amazon.com

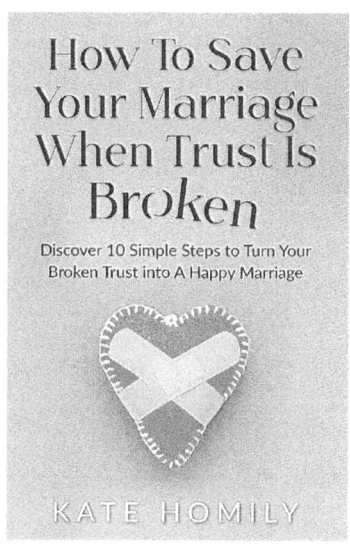

MY FREE GIFT TO YOU: As my way of saying thanks for buying 'The Perfect Relationship Anxiety Workbook for Married Couples' I'd like to give you a FREE COPY of my book 'Keeping Love and Healthy Relationship Alive'

>>> Click Here To Get The Free Book Instantly<<<

The above book is is a gift, given to you as a sincere thanks for buying my e-book. I hope it helps you increase of your life. Download this **FREE BOOK** by clicking the link here

So click the link above to get access now and thanks once again for your support.

Enjoy!

Disclaimer

No part of this e-book may be reproduced or transmitted in any forms of whatsoever, electronic, or mechanical photocopying, recording, or by ay informational storage or retrieval system without express writer, dated and signed permission from the author.

from various sources. Please consult a licensed professional before attempting any techniques outlined in this book.

By reading this document, the reader agrees that under no circumstances is the author responsible for any losses, direct or indirect, that are incurred as a result of the use of the information contained within this document, including, but not limited to, errors, omissions, or inaccuracies.

Table of Contents

Introduction

If you want a marriage that lasts, you need to have trust that lasts. The statement is simple, but what it takes to get there has proven to be challenging for some couples to handle. Marriage isn't always going to be easy, but it's through the hard work you put into it that you will gain all of the love and benefits that you deserve. When thinking about the trust that you have with your partner, consider what you have been through in your relationship. Each action that was taken, choice that was made, and word that was spoken has led you to this moment right now. It isn't uncommon for trust to be broken between married couples because it is so fragile to begin with. With the help of this guide, you are going to learn how to work together and rebuild your trust.

The trust that you share with your significant other is the foundation of your entire relationship. It allows you to work together as partners, to make decisions that benefit the overall health of the relationship. When this trust has been broken, it can leave you feeling lost and confused. The main concept of marriage is unity, coming together to be the very best that you both can be. Many couples destroy the trust in their marriage and do not know how to fix it. Instead of making it a priority, they try to continue on like normal. This is one of the worst things that can be done. A problem that is not addressed in any marriage is bound to come back to the surface eventually.

When you don't address your issues with your partner, or if you don't work hard to solve them, they can lead you to develop resentment for one another. Not having a good sense of trust is something that can make any relationship feel unstable and uncertain. When you are with your partner, you should always feel as though you are being heard and accepted for who you are. With built-up resentment, you are going to begin lashing out at one another. This behavior can become very toxic, causing you to fight a lot and causing your trust to deteriorate even further.

There are many long-term benefits that you will experience as a couple when you learn how to trust one another. Even if you believe that your level of trust is okay for now, it doesn't hurt to take proactive steps to strengthen it. For many couples, rebuilding trust is something that is necessary. Over time, there are many things that can change within the relationship. People hurt one another all the time, both intentionally and unintentionally. Life can be unpredictable in this sense, but your marriage does not have to be. Learning how to address these issues will allow you to finally put them to rest and work on rebuilding your trust.

When you can give your partner the love that they desire, there will be less room for hurting one another and for falling victim to misconceptions. With the ability to communicate openly and an awareness for one another's needs, you and your partner will both feel happy in your marriage. You will learn how to avoid betrayal, preserving the trust that you already share between you. By placing a priority on this, you are showing one another that you both care deeply about the relationship. No matter how long you have been together, there is never a moment in your marriage where you should stop trying. It is the persistent action of putting in effort that will allow you both to keep going strong.

To better understand your spouse, you need to understand their love language. This means that there are certain behaviors and actions that they are going to be most responsive to. As you deepen your relationship, you should pay attention to these things. Not everyone defines intimacy in the same way. For some, this action is very physical. For others, receiving gifts is an intimate act. You need to learn about what your partner enjoys and what makes them feel good. This is how you are going to stay on top of their happiness. As you are trying to discover their love language, make sure that you are also open about your own. When your partner does something for you that you enjoy, be sure to let them know.

Regardless of how long you have been married, you should never stop communicating. When you can continually validate your partner and let them know that they are doing great, this is going to keep the boundaries very clear. In addition, you must speak up when your partner does something that hurts you. Instead of assuming that they will realize this has happened, be direct with them. Explain exactly what you are feeling and why. There is no need to blame them or shame them, but do let them know when their behavior directly affects you. In some cases, they might not even realize that they're hurting you.

This guide is going to help you with all aspects of communication. From establishing a love language to telling your partner when you have reached your limit, these things are very important to making your marriage last. You are going to learn exercises and strategies that will help you both as a couple. It is natural to need a recovery period after your trust has been broken, but this does not mean that you can't get back to a healthy marriage. It's going to take effort and it's likely going to take time, but you need to be willing to see it through. Work together and talk about the things that matter most to you. Express your love for one another in the best ways that you know how. If you ever begin to feel stuck, refer to the tips that you are about to learn and enjoy your newly repaired marriage.

Chapter 1:

What Happens to Love

After We Are in a

Relationship?

Love evolves just as people do. When you first started dating your partner, it's likely that the sparks were flying. You probably wanted to be around one another 24/7 and were excited to learn more about each other. This is the way that most relationships begin, and this stage is known as the "honeymoon" stage. It is thought that, after some time, you will begin to see one another's flaws. The end of this stage can be a very big make-it-or-break-it point in your relationship because you will begin to see one another for who you truly are. In a healthy relationship, it won't matter when the honeymoon stage ends because the love you have for each other will still remain. You should both be appreciative of one another, all qualities included.

Deciding that you want to get married is a very big milestone in life. This means that you've found the person you want to be with forever. In your commitment to your spouse, you are acknowledging that you are going to be there for them no matter what. However, it becomes easy to find flaws in one another after some time has gone by. Things that used to be minor annoyances can easily grow into major problems if the couple is unable to communicate and reach a solution. Many couples lose sight of the love that they originally found because they're quick to start bickering or blow things out of proportion and get into arguments. Getting back to the root of your love will help you remember that you can still have that honeymoon feeling, even after several years.

Keeping the Flame Lit

Your love should be treated as something precious and rare. It can be hard to think about it this way when you already know so much about your partner and their traits. Understand that nobody is perfect, yourself included. There are always going to be small things that get on your nerves, but at the end of the day, you should remember why you are with your significant other. You need to remember why you chose one another out of all the other people that you could've been with. This is what keeps your marriage special and is something that only the two of you could ever understand. Make sure that you're doing your part in keeping the sparks flying when you're with one another.

The following are some ways that you can aim to bring the romance back into your relationship:

- **Have Alone Time** - For many couples, getting adequate alone time can be difficult. Between work and kids, the amount of time that you get to spend on your marriage is likely limited. It's important that you make this time, though. Anything that is worth putting in effort for will be something that you can make time for. Schedule it on your calendar if you need to. Go on dates with one another and rekindle the feelings that you had when you first met. Being able to enjoy this quality time will showcase all of the things that you first noticed about your partner, what made you fall in love with them.

- **Focus on Intimacy** - Life gets busy and that is no secret. No matter how busy you are, you need to make time for intimacy. That said, the number of times you have sex isn't going to indicate how successful your marriage is. It should be something that you do because you have passion for your partner and you want to make them feel good. Scheduled sex can become boring and routine. Take your partner by surprise by showing them some extra initiative. Be more daring and try new things. A little excitement in the bedroom is one of many ways that you can rekindle your spark.

- **Work with Tension** - All couples are going to have tension between them at times. You aren't carbon copies of one another, so you are bound to get into disagreements. Instead of working to immediately diffuse this tension, let it play out. Sometimes, passion can arise from tension. Hear one another out and realize why the tension is being created. Once you have a better understanding of this, you might be able to channel it into something positive. No married couple should live without having at least a few disagreements from time to time. Having different opinions is healthy and should be celebrated.

- **Change Your Routine** - Almost all married couples have a routine that they have fallen into. This can include everything from what time they wake up to what they typically eat for dinner. Any routine can become boring or tiresome after a while. If you want to keep your relationship exciting, it's necessary to change this routine occasionally. You don't have to completely take apart the schedule that you share, but try doing things that are more spontaneous. Take your spouse on a surprise date one night or buy them a random gift to show your appreciation. It's little things like these that can really add some passion to your relationship.

- **Practice Emotional Vulnerability** - You need to be open with your partner and this includes being open about your emotions, as well. Many couples find it challenging to be open in this way, but it's necessary if you want your partner to know exactly how you're feeling. They should be the person you go to when you have good news, bad news, or anything in between. Work on opening up more, showing your partner that you trust them when you're in a vulnerable state of being. This can become a mutually beneficial action that brings the two of you closer together.

How to Handle Conflict

As mentioned, conflict is going to happen between yourself and the person that you love. It is inevitable, a part of any marriage. What matters most is your ability to address it and deal with it. When you are married, you need to understand that your actions can impact your partner without you even realizing it. You've agreed to commit to one another in this lifetime, so you need to be mindful of the things that you do. If you upset your partner, whether it was intentional or unintentional, you need to have the patience and the willpower to fix the problem. The longer two people are together, the more likely they are to become lazy when it comes to communicating and problem-solving. In reality, you must work harder than ever as your relationship matures. This is what keeps you both strong.

Negativity

Being negative toward one another is an example of something that causes conflict. Whether you are in a bad mood because of your partner or because of something else, know that bringing negativity into your relationship is not going to end well. When two people who know each other very well begin to argue, this can lead to hurt feelings and even irreversible damage. Make it a conscious decision to find healthy outlets for your negativity. If something is bothering you, do not sit on this information. Instead, speak up about it. You can express your feelings to your partner without blaming them. Explain what you are going through and how they can help you.

By getting rid of any unnecessary negativity in the relationship, you'll both enjoy being around one another more. It isn't fun to enter a room and feel like you can't even sit next to your spouse because of all the tension. You need to work through your issues if you want to move forward from them. Those who don't have the willpower will often become lazy and accept this tension as their new reality. While it has become a cliche to refer to married couples having lots of arguments, your own marriage doesn't have to be this way. You can find harmony and a balanced dynamic with your partner by keeping track of what you do when you're feeling negative.

Before you get into a disagreement with your partner, stop and think about what the underlying issue is. Are they at fault? Is there anything that you can do for yourself before you take this out on them? You are going to experience a lot of trial and error as you begin to navigate through your feelings, but this is normal. What matters most is that you try. When you can identify your feelings and what to do with them before automatically getting into it with your partner, you'll find that it's very beneficial for your relationship. It will also take a lot of the pressure off of you.

Betrayal

Being betrayed by your spouse can be a devastating thing to deal with. No matter what kind of betrayal it was, their actions have caused you to become so upset that you've lost your trust for them. Much like conflicts, it's also important to address and work through betrayals of trust. When they are ignored, they can jeopardize a marriage very quickly. In any instance when you feel betrayed, you need to express this to your spouse. Instead of automatically forgiving them or trying to find a quick solution, you'll need to work together to identify where this behavior stemmed from and how they are going to win your trust back.

Those who are too quick to sweep things under the rug will often find themselves in the same position again later on. There is no easy fix when handling a betrayal, especially one that concerns cheating. If your partner cheats on you, this puts you in a very painful position, and you must decide if you're going to forgive them or end the relationship. It gets messy when so many feelings are involved and tensions are high. Know what you deserve and what you are willing to put up with. Everyone needs to have their own personal limits. For some, cheating is an absolute deal-breaker. For others, cheating can be forgiven over time. You need to decide what makes sense for you and your relationship.

Make it clear to your spouse when you are not on good terms. This leaves less room for misunderstandings. If you're hurt to the point where you no longer think you want to continue in your marriage, you need to tell them. What they do next is going to be very indicative of how much they value the relationship. You should never have to beg someone to be with you or to be good to you. The right partner is going to do this automatically because they want to be with you. Whether you forgive them or not is entirely up to you.

Rebuilding

When you are in the process of rebuilding your marriage, you need to take as much time for yourself as necessary. Do what it takes to make yourself happy and take things day-by-day. Nothing is going to fix itself automatically; it's going to require hard work from both of you. Make sure that your partner understands where you're coming from and why you're upset by their actions. Tell them how you're feeling and let them know that the trust between the two of you will need to be restored before you can continue with a normal relationship dynamic. Own up to anything that you have done on your end. When you can take accountability for your actions, this makes it less likely that blame will be placed on you.

To work on your marriage effectively, you should not be focused on pointing fingers. Instead, you need to focus on your love and how you got to this point. Say that you're sorry when you're in the wrong. Don't delay and don't fall back on excuses. It's better to be entirely honest with your partner than to lead them on with lies. Understand that pain can be very deep sometimes. While they are hurting, they need to know that you are also hurting. Sometimes, an act of betrayal can cause you to look at yourself differently. You may suffer from low self-esteem as a result of being betrayed by your significant other. This becomes a part of the healing process, as you work on ways to get back to the person that you were before this happened.

Avoid defensive behavior. When you are trying to work out your issues, becoming defensive is only going to contribute to your problems. Understand that you might be in the wrong. It can be very hard to admit to these things, but it is necessary. Just as you need to work on doing this, so does your partner. Coming up with excuses is only going to provide you with distractions and prevent you from fixing your actual problems. Accusatory behavior is also commonly seen when couples are trying to rebuild their marriages. When someone does not want to admit that they are in the wrong, they turn the situation around and attack their partner for something. This is very unhealthy behavior and it needs to be monitored.

Acting helpless when you are trying to mend things with your partner is something that should be avoided. This is yet another way for you to avoid taking accountability for your actions. If you notice this behavior in yourself or in your partner, you need to pay attention to it. In any conflict that occurs that results in an argument, you should know that you're both responsible in some way. There was likely no conversation that consisted of only one of you talking and expressing yourself. Acting helpless will not fix anything, and it will not automatically place the blame on the other person. As a couple, you need to both learn how to admit when you were wrong.

Behavior that tends to suppress conflict instead of resolving it can lead to something known as relationship anxiety. This occurs when you feel literal anxiety when thinking of your relationship or of being in a relationship. Even if you've never felt this way before, it's easy to develop these feelings after dealing with stressful situations that are not being resolved. When you get into this state of mind, it can become very damaging for the overall health of your relationship. You might end up feeling like your relationship isn't good enough or that you aren't good enough. A lot of negative feelings tend to pop up when the conflict doesn't get resolved.

Being realistic, no one can simply resolve conflict and immediately go back to feeling happy and fine. Conflict resolution is a process that couples need to master together. It should not be expected that just because you apologize to your partner about something, they will go back to a happy mood with a positive mindset. Hurtful actions and betrayal can take time to get over. Even if you feel okay, that doesn't mean that your partner will automatically feel the same way. Respect their feelings once you have talked about the issues and found solutions. Know that they might need some additional time to process everything.

The best thing that you can do is exercise your patience once you have talked about your conflict and agreed on what you'd both like to do about it. You are each going to have your own unique ways of dealing with this process, so neither one of you can be rushed. It would be unfair of you to take all the time that you needed in order to move forward, yet not give your partner the same treatment. You need to make sure that you're treating them exactly as you would want to be treated. Ask yourself if you would be okay with your own treatment if the roles were reversed.

When you think about all of the different ways that you have shown bias in the past, you might become enlightened about why certain conflicts continue to come back into your lives. When you notice a repeating pattern, this is likely a sign that you aren't truly resolving the conflict. To reach a point of resolution, you must both be willing to move forward from what happened. If there is any resentment or guilt being held on to, then it seems that you need to work on this issue more.

Above all, you need to figure out how to get back to your vulnerability if you want to truly heal your marriage. It can be difficult to convince yourself to be vulnerable with your partner again, especially if they have done something wrong or if you've been betrayed. Keep reminding yourself that this process is going to take time. Be mindful of your own actions as you pay attention to what they're doing on their end. It takes an equal amount of effort if you want to see a real difference. Use your patience and listen to your gut instinct.

Chapter 2:

How to Build Love and Avoid Betrayal in a Relationship

All couples want a happy and harmonious marriage, but how do you know that you and your partner have what it takes? Love is a risk that is taken every single day.

When you love someone, you're willing to put your feelings on the line in order to experience the happiness that love brings into your life. Many people get hurt, even by those who care about them deeply. It can be inevitable sometimes. As a married couple, you need to focus on how to build your love so that it becomes stronger every day. When you have this strength together, you will both be less likely to betray one another. Having a sense of openness with one another can prove to be very helpful.

In this chapter, you are going to learn how to understand one another. When you don't have to do any guessing in your relationship, you're going to be able to provide exactly what your partner needs. Everyone hopes that they're a great spouse, but with these tips, you can make sure that you actually are one. An effort to understand your partner is going to go a long way. Not only will it clarify boundaries and enhance your communication skills as a couple, but you will both feel that more effort is being put into the relationship. The longer that you are together, the more that you should aim to learn about one another. If you stop trying, this is usually when things fall apart.

Love Languages

There are 5 different love languages that most people can identify with. In this section, they will be explained. As you read through each description, see which one you can personally relate to the most. Also, see if you can spot the one that sounds most like your partner. By having this knowledge, you'll be able to know how to handle different aspects of your marriage. If you know what your partner considers an act of love, then you can do your best to express it to them in the way that they know best.

Affirmation

This love language revolves around the idea that positive words can be used to build your partner up. They likely enjoy being complimented and told what you admire most about them. When speaking to a person who identifies with this love language, they'll be much more responsive to positive reinforcement than demands. For example, saying that you appreciate when your partner washes the dishes rather than criticizing them for not washing them is going to result in a much better response.

Gift-Giving

This love language is exactly how it sounds — your partner will enjoy and appreciate when you get them gifts to showcase your love. People who identify with this love language usually have a great appreciation for material items. If they know that you are willing to buy them the things that make them happy, they will feel very loved and cared for. In their eyes, this will show them that you were thinking about them.

Acts of Service

When you do things for your partner without being asked, they will end up feeling very loved. Some examples include doing the laundry, taking care of the grocery shopping, or cleaning up around the house. To a person who values this kind of love, these tasks are the ultimate way to show your consideration. They know that by taking action, you can see how much hard work they usually put into these same tasks. This love language is based around the idea that you are willing to take some of the weight off of their shoulders.

Quality Time

Being able to spend alone time with your spouse is very valuable to a lot of people. Having uninterrupted time together can definitely be a love language, as life tends to become busy for most people. When you can show your partner that you appreciate them enough to want to spend individual time together on a regular basis, this is going to make them feel special. This can range from anything like going out on a date to sitting down on the couch and having a one-on-one conversation.

Physical Touch

This one is a self-explanatory love language. People who value physical touch want as much kissing, hugging, and touching as possible in their relationship. When they are being shown physical intimacy, they feel the most loved. While this might not be the only way to express your love, it proves to be the most important way for those who value physical touch over anything else.

Getting a better understanding of your partner's love language is going to help you communicate with them. As you know, great communication goes beyond talking. You need to learn how to read them, to see what they truly need from you. When you can identify and respect their love language, this shows that you've spent time getting to know them on an even deeper level. It's a misconception that being together for a long time means that you know everything there is to know about one another. You're both constantly evolving, which means that there is always going to be more to learn.

When you're happy in your marriage, you're both going to treat each other better. In the same way that positive energy is contagious, so is having consideration. After showing your significant other that you not only know what their love language is, but are also doing your best to communicate with them in that unique way, they will likely feel inspired to do the same. This can prove to be a time of exponential growth in your marriage. It will show you both that there is always room for improvement as you learn and grow together.

With an effort to treat one another better, you will find that rebuilding your relationship *is* possible, no matter what you have endured. Getting to this point will prove to be the most difficult part, but once you get there, you'll be able to make significant improvements in the health of your marriage. Both of you have to want it and both of you have to put in an equal amount of effort. When one person is trying very hard and the other person is not, this is going to highlight the inequality in your relationship. It is not a good feeling to discover this. Always try to be mindful of your partner's level of effort and make sure that you check-in with one another if you feel that you need to redistribute the balance.

Power Struggles

When reading the term "power struggles," it makes sense that you would assume they are all bad. A struggle has a negative connotation behind it. What you'll learn is that there can be good struggles and bad struggles. Having a little bit of a power struggle in your relationship can prove to be a positive thing, one that brings out more passion. It is normal to feel this way with your partner, as you do almost everything together. There are certain times when you might want to do something in your own way, yet you have to make compromises because of your partner — this is how marriage works.

As you know, once the honeymoon stage is over, you're just left with two individuals who must work together to accept all parts of each other. Not only do you have to make sure that your relationship keeps growing, but you also need to make sure that you are both compatible with one another in the lifestyle that you're living. You should each understand what the other wants to achieve in the relationship. Both of you should feel happy at the end of the day and secure in the relationship. There are many couples who ignore red flags, only to realize that they weren't actually on the same page.

The best thing to do when you notice a power struggle in your relationship, good or bad, is to pay attention to it. See where this tension is stemming from. The difference between the good and the bad is if it allows you to grow as a couple. Any positive power struggle is going to result in growth for your relationship. This type of dynamic might encourage you to push some boundaries with one another, but ultimately, it will allow you to test one another without causing conflicts. This type of tension can be very beneficial when it comes to your passion and excitement in the relationship.

Negative power struggles revolve around control. When you get into this kind of a power struggle with your partner, the result is usually going to be an argument or a fight. Most of the time, manipulation is a component of a negative power struggle. One person will manipulate the other as a way to control their behavior. When they're able to gain this kind of control, they'll feel that they have more power in the relationship. For some, this can be a good feeling. It seems less likely that you'll be hurt when you have more control in the relationship. The problem is that this is not a representation of an equal partnership. This kind of control results in unhealthy behaviors.

In a healthy relationship, there is no need for any one person to be in control. Sometimes, the control is determined naturally because certain people have more dominant personality traits while others prefer to be more submissive. If you feel that your spouse is demanding more control than is typically held by each of you, this could be an indication that there is a negative power struggle taking place. You need to make sure that control doesn't become the focus of your relationship because marriage is so much more than that. It should be about the life that you're living together, not the life that one person dictates.

After you deal with being controlled for a long period of time, you're going to reach your breaking point. This can manifest as an outburst or a sudden urge to resist being controlled. If you feel that you've had enough of this type of behavior, you're justified in wanting to break free from it. A healthy relationship should be functional and harmonious. There should not be a need for one person to control the other and dictate their actions. As a couple, you need to be able to love and appreciate one another for who you truly are.

Use caution if you feel that you are in this kind of situation. It is possible that toxic behavior will evolve into abusive behavior if you are not careful. The instant you begin to feel unsafe or that you are being treated unfairly, it's always best to speak up or get out of this situation. If you wait too long, you might feel that you have no other choice but to stay. Many couples find that their love cannot last once the power has been shifted too far. The person being controlled is bound to grow tired of it, losing sight of their love.

Practice healthy expressions of power. Let one another take turns making decisions and make sure that you are showing respect, no matter who is in charge of the situation. When you can treat one another equally, any power struggle that you encounter will likely be able to evolve into positive tension. With this, you can turn it into passion or even romance. Being able to find the balance with each other can be tough, even if you've already been in the relationship for some time. You need to ensure that you're aware of your own role and to tone it down when you need to.

Openness

The key to building your love as a couple comes from your ability to be open with one another. These are some steps that you can take together to ensure that you are being as open as possible:

- **Get Rid of Your Fears** - When speaking to your partner, remember that this is a person that should not judge you. No matter what is on your mind, you should be able to fully express yourself to your partner without fear of being rejected or ridiculed. If this happens, it's a sign that points to an unhealthy relationship. You'll know that you have to fix something if this occurs. A great marriage involves the ability to bounce ideas off of one another. You should both feel comfortable talking to each other about anything. Try your best to get rid of any fears that you might be holding on to and remind yourself that your partner loves you and cares about what you have to say.

- **Value Honesty** - Honesty is always going to be the best way to approach any topic. When you can be entirely honest with your spouse, you're showing them that you're being transparent. Healthy relationships do not involve having to lie to one another, whether it be to hide wrongdoings or to ensure that no disagreements happen. Couples aren't always going to get along, but a casual disagreement can be healthy for the relationship. If you notice that you feel a need to lie to your partner, you need to question the health of your marriage.

- **Make Statements** - If you want to talk to your partner about something that makes you nervous, it's best to just speak from the heart. Say exactly what you're feeling and do not phrase it as a question. This invalidates your own feelings by asking the other person for input. Stand behind your statement and allow yourself to say exactly what you mean. This is going to help you open up to your partner by encouraging you to commit to what you're telling them.

- **Let Your Feelings and Behavior Align** - When you tell your partner that you feel a certain way, your actions should be representative of this. Passive-aggressive behavior stems from behavior that doesn't align with feelings that have been expressed. For example, when you tell your partner that you're fine, you don't need to give them the cold shoulder. Speak up when something is actually bothering you and be aware of your actions. If you need some time to collect your thoughts and calm down before discussing something, let them know.

- **Ask for What You Want** - Your spouse cannot read your mind. No matter how well you're getting along, your thoughts are unique. Hinting for things that you want might just leave you feeling upset when your partner doesn't follow through. Be direct and expressive. If you seek something, ask your partner for it. This is a good rule to follow for anything from material items to intimacy. When you're direct, you won't be left feeling disappointed when your partner doesn't pick up on the hints.

- **Have an Open Dialogue** - Try to be expressive when you communicate with one another. If your spouse is telling you something important, it's likely that they want your feedback. Avoid short, one-word answers. Think about how you feel and express yourself openly. It can become frustrating when one person is expressive and the other is only reacting with basic small talk. Your level of communication needs to be on par if you'd like to open up to one another.

It sounds simplistic, yet it's true — if you can be open to romance and intimacy as a couple, you're going to be happier together. As more arguments happen and fights occur, it can become hard to remember the things that first brought the two of you together. Making a relationship last has a lot to do with reminiscing. Whether you are thinking about fond memories that you've shared or how much you've grown together, these things can allow you to feel closer and will remind you that you need to be seeking out new ways to love one another.

In an ideal marriage, you should be able to share every part of yourself with your partner. While you're entitled to your own privacy, there shouldn't be any topics that are considered off-limits because you're afraid that they'll result in an argument or a betrayal. Stability is a very valuable trait that you should seek when you're with your partner. If they can make you feel safe and secure, then you are likely going to be able to open up to them more and vice versa.

It is possible to restore your love after it has been tarnished. If both of you are willing to focus on positivity and figuring out how to help the relationship grow, then you're going to be met with positive results. When you enter anything with a negative mindset, you aren't going to see the results that you truly want. Your mind and your intentions have to align. Show one another that happiness is a priority that you share in the relationship.

Chapter 3:

The Love He/She Desires

Most

When you can figure out the kind of love that your partner needs to feel happy, you're halfway to making a difference in the quality of your marriage. Being able to determine the love language is only the first step, though. The next step includes taking action and giving your spouse exactly what they need. Through your thoughtfulness and attention to detail, you'll be able to give them the love that they deserve. This is the part of the relationship that will require a lot of hard work, but it's all worth it in order to know that your spouse is happy to be with you. In a relationship that has balance, you'll be receiving the same treatment.

As you know, you cannot become lazy with the way that you express your love for your partner. The same gifts and dates aren't always going to be as impactful as time goes on. This also suggests that you are taking a lazy approach. To put real effort into your relationship, you need to show your partner that you're constantly evaluating their input. You need to show them that you're always paying attention to them and to their needs. Relationships evolve over time and it's normal to experience changes in the way that you express your love for one another and in the way you'd like to be loved.

Acting on Love Languages

In this section, you're going to learn specific ways that you can show your partner you care. Because each one is unique, you need to have a good idea of the actions that fall into each category. With more experience, you will be able to flawlessly shower your partner with love, resulting in a very positive outcome for your relationship. Everyone enjoys feeling special, especially when it is their partner that is helping them feel this way. Once you've gotten a feeling for the types of actions your partner likes, you can get creative and come up with even more ways to make them feel special.

Ways to Practice Affirmation

- Tell your partner you're proud of them
- Compliment their appearance
- Express how hard-working they are
- Acknowledge all that they do around the house
- Remind them of their great qualities
- Support their goals
- Offer emotional guidance

Words are the most powerful way to show your love to a partner who enjoys affirmation. Know that what you say is very important to them. For this reason, you need to be especially mindful of how you express yourself. Your partner is going to crave compliments and encouragement. Make sure that you give this to them frequently in order to show them that you respect their love language.

When you do something that upsets your partner, an apology is going to mean a lot to them. They are going to want you to express yourself and acknowledge what you did wrong. When the situation is reversed, you can expect your partner to be very open about what you did that upset them. This trait is not meant to make you feel bad, but to encourage open communication with one another.

Just because you feel that your partner should already know how you feel about them doesn't mean that you should stop telling them. At the beginning of your relationship, you likely gave them many compliments. The more comfortable you get in the relationship, the easier it becomes to stop giving compliments. You might still feel the exact same way about your partner, but you shouldn't assume that they know this. Imagine that you're telling them for the first time each time that you compliment them.

When you can make affirmations a big part of your dynamic, it will allow your partner to feel important in the exact way that they crave. With a little bit of attention to detail, you'll find that your relationship will effortlessly blossom in a natural way. Many couples become frustrated when they feel that they have to force compliments or express kindness. In order to avoid this, make sure that you are always speaking from your heart. Tell your partner exactly how you feel about them.

Ways to Practice Gift-Giving

- Make them something by hand
- Buy them an experience
- Get them something unexpected
- Buy them something that they mentioned to you
- Surprise them with their favorite food

There isn't much to explain about gift-giving because it can be pretty straightforward when you have a partner who prefers it as their love language. Those who do feel cared for when they receive gifts from their partners. It's a representation of you thinking about them and deciding to get them something that will make them happy. To some, the idea of using material items to express love can seem questionable, but you should know that there are also other ways that you can give your partner gifts.

For example, making something for your partner by hand can be a nice touch. Instead of simply going to the store and buying them something, you can get creative and come up with an idea of something that you can craft yourself. This kind of gift becomes even more meaningful because it's one-of-a-kind. A letter can also be considered a gift. Sit down and write your spouse a detailed letter about how you feel about them. This is another way that you can change up the norm of going to the store and simply buying them something.

The element of surprise becomes useful in this love language. If your partner isn't expecting a gift from you, this gesture can prove to be exciting and thoughtful. Surprise them with little things frequently. Remember that a gift does not have to be expensive or elaborate in order to be appreciated. You know your partner best, so you'll have an idea of what you can get for them based on their current interests. Make sure to keep in mind ideas such as what they've liked to eat recently, any movies that they've been wanting to see, or any new places that they've been wanting to visit. You can buy material items as well as experiences.

Know that your relationship should never revolve solely around you buying your partner gifts. A common misconception of this love language is that the other person will not be happy in the relationship unless they are constantly being showered with gifts. Part of what makes gift-giving so special is that it comes from the heart. No matter what you decide to give your partner, you put thought into it and that is meaningful. Your small, homemade gift is going to be just as valued as a piece of jewelry.

Ways to Practice Acts of Service

- Take care of the household chores
- Go grocery shopping
- Assemble furniture
- Get an oil change for the car
- Organize and clean the closet

You can show your partner kindness in many ways by doing a helpful act of service for them. Those who speak this love language value your hard work. No matter what kind of service you do for them, they are likely going to take this as a sign that you're observant and committed to the relationship. By putting in this effort to complete a task, you are demonstrating to your partner that you're willing to take on some of the work. This is the way that an ideal relationship should function.

If you don't speak the same love language, you probably underestimate the thought that goes into doing simple tasks such as washing a load of laundry or washing the dishes. To your partner, however, these tasks mean a lot. Knowing that they're getting a little bit of extra help will allow them to feel that they're being valued. It's never a good feeling when you know you're pulling more of the weight. This love language promotes balance in relationships.

Much like the other love languages, your gestures don't have to be extravagant in order for them to count. Something as simple as opening the car door can be considered an act of service to your partner. This is a very small task that you likely don't think much about, but realize that your partner could be very positively impacted by it. Another example is when you consider their needs as you're doing something for yourself. If you stop off at the store for something to drink, getting your partner something to drink as well will show them that you were thinking of them.

You don't have to do much to make your partner happy. There is no need to try and take over every chore and task because this will eventually lead your partner to believe that you don't need their help. Much like the idea that goes behind gift-giving, you don't want to speak this love language too frequently or else it will no longer feel special. Do things for your partner because you truly want to and you are feeling inspired to do so. Also, don't feel limited to expressing your love using a single love language all the time, as many partners like to feel loved in more than one way.

Ways to Practice Quality Time
- Go on more dates
- Spend time together without distractions
- Take drives together
- Brainstorm with one another
- Make important decisions together

It seems that most couples agree — more quality time together would be welcomed. To those who speak this love language, quality time is a must. Life tends to get busy, but this does not mean that your quality time together as a couple should be reduced. When something is truly important to you, this means that you should be able to make time for it. In order to effectively communicate in this love language, you need to be great at prioritizing your time. You might need to adjust your time management skills if being too busy is what's stopping you from spending more time together.

Understand that quality time is not the same as simply being around each other. You are likely around your spouse a lot, but what turns this into quality time is the undivided attention that you give to one another. Being distracted by your surroundings or electronic devices is going to take away the meaning from this time that you have. Make sure that you are present when you have the opportunity to enjoy quality time together. Put your phone on silent and go somewhere that you and your partner can be alone.

No matter if you are talking casually or discussing something of importance, what happens during this time is so special because only the two of you share it. If you were to share these intimate moments with others, this can be considered a betrayal by your spouse. Make sure that you're always focused on what is going on in front of you. Your partner will appreciate it and you'll be able to get a lot more out of the time that you spend together.

Ways to Practice Physical Touch
- Hold hands more often
- Spend time in the morning cuddling

- Initiate intimacy when you feel sparks between you
- Spontaneously kiss them
- Place your hand on their back when you are standing near one another

This love language is very straightforward. If your partner enjoys physical intimacy, you should know the basics of what you can do in order to show them love. The one thing that can stand in the way of expressing this is if you don't enjoy physical intimacy as much as your partner does. If you aren't in the mood to touch them or kiss them, this can send signals to them that you don't care about them as much as you once did. Be careful with how you express your love to them and make sure that you are only initiating physical intimacy when you feel the same way.

The best thing that you can do to speak this love language is to listen to your heart. Get close to your partner, both physically and emotionally. Act in a natural way based on the chemistry that you feel between the two of you. If you have a partner who speaks this love language, then you likely have intense physical chemistry. You might have to find ways to reignite this passion the longer that you're with your partner. As you know, intimacy can slow down for couples who have been together for some time, but it doesn't have to.

Never schedule your intimacy. This can cause it to feel forced or ingenuine. You should make time for these moments with your partner because you want to, not because you feel that you have to in order to speak their love language. Acting spontaneously can be a great way to feel the passion once again. It will remind the two of you what it was that first attracted you to one another. Getting back to these feelings is a very healthy thing for couples to do. It can make any trivial issues that you're going through seem like not as big of a deal when you're reminded of how physically compatible you are together. Listen to their signals. Their body language is going to tell you a lot about what they want you to do next.

The Importance of Respect

When you and your partner share a mutual respect for one another, this is going to provide you with a strong foundation for your marriage. In order to determine if you have respect, you must first define it. Ask yourself what respect means to you. For some, it means having a deep admiration for one another. There is no right or wrong answer because what matters most is that you both share the same opinion on what defines respect. A general overview of respect between partners states that one person should not have authority over the other. This eliminates control issues and promotes individual thinking while maintaining kindness and compassion for one another.

To get a general idea of where you both stand, take a look at how you treat each other on a daily basis. Do you help each other when you're in need? Do you do things for your partner without being asked? If you do these things, they are both signs that you're showing your respect regularly. Your partner can ask you for respect, but they shouldn't have to. It should be something that you want to do because you care and because you love them. In turn, your partner should show their respect for you in a similar way. If anything feels forced, then respect is something that you will likely have to work on together. When respect is forced, this is usually an indication of something unresolved standing in your way.

As you know, unresolved issues can play a big role in your relationship. This is why it's important not to sweep your fights under the rug. You need to talk about them and then discuss ways to make changes for the better. If you continue to do the same things over and over again, you're going to be met with the same results. No one enjoys frequently fighting with their significant other. This is draining and upsetting. Living in harmony is much more desirable. Point out any unresolved issues that you notice when you're gauging the respect you have for one another. Some serious conversations might have to take place before you can go on any further.

Because no relationship is perfect, there might be several things for you to discuss and work out. Don't feel bad about this. Know that each step you take toward clarity, you are taking another step toward having mutual respect. Do your best to have these discussions in a way that is not accusatory because this might just reignite the fight once again. Know that what has already happened cannot be changed, but your actions going forward can be. When you are both able to let go of the things that are bothering you, there is going to be a lot more room for progress. Holding on to negativity, no matter how trivial it may seem, will always find a way to impact your relationship.

If you want to practice acts of respect, you can apply the following to your marriage:

- **Listen to Each Other** - Sometimes, communication isn't going to be about talking. Make sure that you listen to your spouse when they need to express their feelings. You don't always have to think of what to say or how to relate the conversation back to your own feelings. Being an active listener can be very valuable, making your spouse feel that you care deeply about their well-being. Before you respond, ask yourself if you're speaking to add to the conversation or if you're speaking to make the conversation about you.

- **Work on Compromising** - All couples need to be efficient at compromising. There are going to be many instances where you'll want different things, yet you'll have to find a middle ground to keep you both happy. Being able to let go of your original thought or desire can be tough, especially if you're a naturally stubborn person. It takes a lot of communication and effort to be able to come to a middle ground with your partner, but it's necessary if you want a healthy marriage.

- **Give Each Other Space** - This step might seem counter-productive, but it's actually essential if you want to build your respect. When you're constantly around each other, it becomes easier to feel irritable. You are both individuals and you both deserve some time to yourself. When you're apart, this will show you what you're missing when the other person is not around. This can work out in your favor by showing you all of the great aspects that your spouse brings to your life.

- **Honor All Boundaries** - All couples should have a healthy set of boundaries in place. No matter how much you love one another and how close you are in your relationship, you need to remember that you are two separate people with different limits. When you have boundaries that are to be followed, this is a great way to build respect. Your boundaries are going to be different and that is exactly what will promote you to be mindful of one another's feelings.

Chapter 4:

The Secret to Loving Your

Spouse Effectively

When you have a strong bond of love, you are going to be able to grow your marriage into something that is happy, successful, and beneficial. It can be hard to remember to focus on the love that you share when your thoughts are clouded by betrayal, confusion, or disagreements that you've experienced with your spouse. When you hurt one another, it takes time for you both to heal. This is going to happen because it is inevitable in all partnerships. You're trusting one another every single day in a big way. By giving your partner your heart, you're showing them that you're willing to take a risk. You know that they want the best for you, but you're also acknowledging that you know you might get hurt.

Love is uncertain, but that is what makes it beautiful. You cannot predict when your partner is going to do something that will upset you. What you can do, however, is learn how to get back to the love that you share no matter what. When it comes to betrayal, you both need to figure out what your breaking point is. Understand that not all negativity can be fixed. If you hurt one another to a point of no return, there is not going to be any hope of reviving the relationship. You need to determine that you are both on the same page, that you both want to make the marriage work.

When you're able to do this, you will be able to love one another in the way that you both need most. You will know when to be there for one another and when to give space. These things cannot be learned overnight, but if you are always making progress, you are going to become a better spouse in the process. Eliminate the idea that certain issues cannot be fixed. This is only true when one or both of you are unwilling to fix them. Remember that it takes two in any aspect of any relationship. When you can both agree that you value your love enough to save it, then you can start to make some progress.

Discover Key Issues

All relationships have certain issues that seem to repeat themselves. These are known as key issues because they seem to remain unresolved. If you notice that a lot of your fights stem from a single topic, it is safe to say that you have found one of your key issues. Examine what your last 5 fights were about. Have a discussion with your partner on what you each believe you were fighting about, down to the very root of the problem. This can become an eye-opening experience in more than one way. You'll be able to see certain patterns in your marriage and you'll also be able to see if you perceive these fights in the same way.

You'd be surprised to discover how many issues you're both misunderstanding, causing more fights in your relationship. When you have misunderstandings that are never clarified, you might be fighting over something that you unknowingly feel the same way about. Realize when you're both saying the same thing in your own unique ways. Many couples don't take the time to break this down and truly examine what is going on in their relationship. This kind of tedious work is necessary if you'd like to see improvement. If you are unclear about where your partner stands on an issue, clarify this by asking them directly. It's better to hear this from their own mouth rather than making assumptions or jumping to conclusions.

Pay attention to anger levels. If the two of you cannot have a serious conversation without resorting to anger, you'll both need to independently work on ways to find outlets for it. When you don't have a way to express your anger and frustration, you're going to end up taking it out on one another. This can prove to be a very big problem in a relationship. It can make your communication seem very unstable and unpredictable. Do your part by making sure that you take a few deep breaths before you express an opinion that differs from your partner's. Try not to think about one of you as right and the other as wrong. Instead, express yourself and listen to what your partner would like to express. Approaching your conversations in this way will lead to much more productive results.

Complaining can come very naturally in a relationship because you are both very comfortable with one another. Be careful that it doesn't become too much of a focus, though. Hearing your partner complain can be very disheartening, especially when it seems like nothing you do is good enough for them. Be mindful of how much you are complaining, as well. If you cannot come up with a solution to the problem, then nothing is going to be resolved. While complaining can feel like a much-needed relief, you need to realize that this can become taxing behavior. Your partner might feel blamed for these things when you don't mean to make them feel this way. It's better to work through your issues on your own when you can before bringing them into any arguments or disagreements.

When you feel like blaming your partner during an argument, stop to think before you speak. Ask yourself what blaming them would do. Would it help the situation? Most of the time, it's only going to add fuel to the fire. If you aren't careful, constant blaming can eventually turn into abusive behavior. When your relationship gets to this point, it's bound to become toxic. No one deserves to be constantly blamed for things, especially when they aren't doing anything wrong. By taking accountability for your actions and being able to communicate, you and your spouse should be able to get rid of the need to place the blame on anyone and focus on the solutions.

Keep in mind that force is never the answer. When you use force or aggression to try and solve your problems, this creates more tension. You need to be mindful of this because you should always be focused on making peace with your issues and solving problems as you become aware of them. Marriage does not have to be difficult. While you are going to run into disagreements, you don't have to let them change your relationship. What you can do is learn and grow from them.

Also, know that men and women interpret information differently. Women are usually able to access their emotions more easily, while men like to rely on rationalization. Of course, this isn't always the case because everyone is different. However, it is something to keep in mind when you feel frustrated. Your spouse might see the exact same situation and react very differently because that is what they're driven to do. Take some time to learn where they're coming from and why they've reacted in this way before judging them for it.

How to Avoid Negativity

1. **Leave Jealousy Behind** - Jealousy is a large contributor to negative energy in relationships. When one or both of you are jealous, this can cause outbursts and arguments. You both need to be secure in yourselves and in your love so you can avoid distortions in your judgment. Couples who are fueled by jealousy will fall into a pattern of toxic accusatory behavior that should be avoided. It can be tough to let go of your jealousy, but remind yourself that you are the one your partner has chosen. Both of you have made a commitment to one another, so the other people around you should not be able to break down your relationship.

2. **Don't Try to Change Them** - You are with your spouse because you fell in love with the qualities that they possess. When you become more comfortable with one another, it can be tempting to try to guide each other toward the behavior that you favor. Know that when you get into the habit of doing this, you're going to start believing that you can change your partner. Because it's a partnership and not a dictatorship, you don't get to have that kind of control over them. You need to make sure that you're in the relationship for the right reasons and that you love them for who they are. If

something bothers you, speak up about it. It is then up to your partner to make any changes that they see fit.

3. **Laugh Together** - It sounds cheesy, but laughter really is the best medicine. When you can laugh with your spouse, this shows that you know how to have fun together. It's important that you don't always take your relationship too seriously because this can cause tension. Understand that there is a time and place for that. You need to be able to feel comfortable enough with one another to laugh things off sometimes. Joke around and keep them amused, especially when the mood is lighthearted. When you do this more often, you'll be reminded that not every moment of tension needs to turn into an argument. Most can work themselves out and be laughed about when you look back on them.

4. **Don't Pick Apart Flaws** - Your partner is likely already aware of their flaws and insecurities. There is no reason to pick them apart any further. Imagine if they were to do the same thing to you. As you can imagine, this would probably be very hurtful. Know that neither one of you is perfect, so you don't need to bring this up during a heated moment. A person's flaws do not make up the entirety of who they are, so it's unfair to use this against them. Learn how to let this go.

5. **Don't Ignore Each Other** - It can be very tempting to resort to the cold shoulder when you aren't getting along, but you should definitely avoid this. Not only is this not a healthy way to resolve your issues, but it can turn into a lasting habit. When you don't address your problems, you'll have a tendency to keep ignoring them until they build up and become worse. It's easier to talk about your problems when they're still fresh on your brain. This will ensure that you're able to get to the root of what is bothering you. It can be easy to forget these things when they're ignored, and this can allow them to compound into larger issues that draw you apart from your partner.

By staying calm, you're going to make sure that any negativity you experience does not escalate into a problem. Working on ways to diffuse your temper is important, especially for your marriage. Learn to recognize when you're becoming angry and take a moment to calm down. When you can calm yourself down before you get angry and reactionary, it will allow you to talk through your problems with your partner instead of yelling at one another. Anger never solves anything fully, so know that resorting to it is only going to mean that you'll have to talk about the issue again. It is better to discuss things right then and there in an effort to get to a solution.

While you can be passionate about many issues, ask yourself if it's worth it to argue with your spouse. You might feel that you have a point to make, but consider if there are other ways to do it. By thinking before you speak, you can avoid saying something hurtful that would otherwise come out when you're in a heated argument. These words might not be how you really feel, but they can leave lasting damage to your relationship if you're not careful. This will likely make the problem escalate into something worse rather than resolving it.

Conflict-Resolution Skills

Do

- **Learn to Agree to Disagree** - When you're having a discussion with your spouse, know that you don't always have to agree on everything. This isn't realistic, nor is it healthy. It's a good thing to be able to have your own opinions. In order to get along better as a couple, what must happen is the ability to respect one another. Even if you don't agree with your spouse, learn how to see their side of things and understand where they're coming from. A little bit of respect goes a long way.
- **Work on Things Now** - Instead of waiting to talk about your issues until they pile up, address them as they come up. A big problem that couples face is when certain issues are only brought up when one person starts to feel

overwhelmed. This can sometimes come across as a surprise to the other person because it was not addressed sooner. Avoid this by saying what's on your mind as you're feeling it. Know that it's always better to talk sooner rather than later.

- **Make Time to Talk** - If something is important to your relationship, you will make time for it. When discussing something you're arguing about, make sure that you set aside at least 30 minutes of uninterrupted time to discuss it. If the conversation needs to be longer, make sure that you're both able to take a break to regroup. When you give your conversations structure, they'll feel less overwhelming and difficult. Understand that you should both be given equal time to talk about how you feel.

- **Examine Your Unmet Needs** - It's often the needs that aren't being met that cause problems. Identify if you have any unmet needs and then bring them up to your partner. This doesn't always have to be a bad thing. Relationships evolve and people change, but as long as you keep each other in the loop, you can maintain a healthy and functional relationship. Know that your needs are valid and important. You deserve to feel happiness, so let your partner know what they can do to make you happy. In turn, your partner should do the same so that you'll know what you can do for them.

- **Brainstorm Solutions Together** - You aren't always going to have the right solution, but sometimes you might. Work together with your spouse to explore several different solutions until you both agree on one. What might seem like the right one to you might not be the right one to them. In order to truly resolve a conflict, you both need to feel at ease. Remember this the next time you feel so certain that you've come up with a solution.

- **Pause for Anger** - If you start to feel like you're losing your temper, take a break. Your argument doesn't have to push you to a breaking point, so don't let it. Use your self-discipline to recognize when your temper is flaring up. Take a moment to walk around outside or to go to a different room so that you can clear your head. Remember to take deep breaths and to identify what is making you so angry. After you regroup, go back to your partner and try to approach the issue like you want to solve it rather than fuel it.

Don't

- Have discussions when you're tired
- Use the words "always" or "never"
- Bring up the opinions of others

- Switch topics to fit your point
- Make judgments about their behavior
- Think your partner can read your mind
- Interrupt your partner while they're speaking
- Bring up past issues to make a point
- Compromise your standards to end the argument

Having an idea of what to do and what not to do will make you an effective problem-solver. This is an essential skill for anyone who is in a long-term relationship. You're going to argue with your spouse, but this doesn't have to mean that your marriage will be damaged in the process. With the help of these tips, you'll both be able to get your points across and come to the conclusion that works best for your relationship.

Through having an open discussion about your problems, you'll both be able to feel seen in the relationship. This can be enough to restore the faith that you once lost, reminding you that you're still with the person that is best for you. All couples are going to experience difficulties throughout their marriages, so it's essential to practice these skills whenever possible. Remember, if you haven't worked on communication skills like these before, it can take some practice to become good at them. Learn how to forgive one another and always try to return to the loving bond that you've worked so hard to create. No one else can fix your problems but the two of you, so it's important that you work together.

Chapter 5:

The Secret to

Unconditional Love That

Couples Need, Yet Few

Find

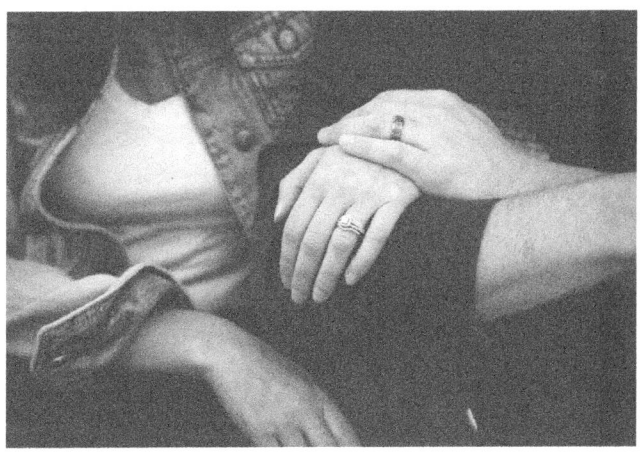

All relationships aren't created equal. You likely know this because of first-hand experience. Think about all of the people that you had to date before you found your spouse. They changed things for you, showed you what true love is supposed to look like. When you decide that you want to marry someone, this is the ultimate display of trust and devotion. It can be hard to get back to this feeling after enduring so many hardships with your spouse. That is the definition of unconditional love, though. It's the ability to still love and care for one another, in spite of any arguments or betrayals that happen over time.

This chapter is devoted to the topic of helping your relationship grow. When you've learned how to love one another unconditionally, you'll be able to enter a stage of growth that will be beneficial for you as an individual and for your relationship. So many people want a love that lasts forever, yet they don't treat their significant other in a way that reflects this. You need to show your partner what you want. Lead by example and there will never be any confusion about where your heart is.

Navigating Your Differences

One-Sided Effort

When one person puts in more effort than the other, this is going to cause problems. You need to work together as a couple to identify if there is an imbalance going on. If you feel that you're putting in more effort than your partner, bringing this issue up can be tricky. You likely don't want to bring this up in a confrontational way because this can lead directly to an argument.

Focus on how this makes you feel. Figure out a way to tell your spouse that you desire more from them. Before you bring this issue to their attention, think about what you would personally like to change about the situation. If you could think about one thing that would make you feel better about it, what would it be? This will prevent you from going into the conversation with an accusatory tone.

If you feel that you aren't pulling your weight, or if your partner has brought this to your attention, do your best to not immediately punish yourself. There is no use in doing this because it will not solve the problem. Instead, you need to think about actionable steps that you can take to improve the situation. Think about how you can be more present for your partner.

There will always be an effective way to solve a problem like this when you're willing to do the work that needs to be done. You must also be willing to listen to what your partner has to say. Nobody is perfect, so it can be a humbling experience to learn exactly what it's going to take to make a difference. Listen to this closely and be open to your partner's feedback.

Emotional Responses

In general, women tend to be more emotional than men. There are exceptions, of course, but this is how it typically is in a relationship. No matter what role you play, understand that your partner might not be as comfortable with expressing their emotions on the same level that you express yours. A problem that can often arise between couples is when one person blames the other for not feeling enough/feeling too much.

Before you become frustrated with your partner because of this, realize that there are many factors that can contribute to their emotional expressiveness. Childhood is one of the first ones. The way that your partner grew up taught them how they should deal with their emotions. Some people are taught healthy forms of expression while others are told that they need to keep their emotions inside. Be mindful of this.

Another factor comes from the way that coping mechanisms are developed. There are unhealthy coping mechanisms that can become a big part of the way that emotions are handled. This can include the suppression of difficult situations and use of aggression to release anger. Your partner might have developed some unhealthy coping mechanisms due to the life experiences that they've lived.

Do your best to meet your partner halfway with emotional expressiveness. If they aren't as open as you are, be gentle with them. It might be hard for them to open up right away. If they are more open than you are, understand that you have every right to say that you aren't there yet if you're struggling to be on the same emotional wavelength. When you can be clear about exactly what you're feeling, this will give your partner all of the insight that they need.

Reservations

A person can become reserved for a wide variety of reasons. This tends to cause problems in a relationship because it can often come across as if your partner doesn't fully trust you when they choose to be reserved. Much like the above example, your partner can have reservations for a wide variety of reasons that have nothing to do with you. From their upbringing to past situations that have impacted them, all of these things come into play.

Don't allow their behavior to lead you to create suspicions. This is a form of jumping to conclusions and it's not likely to work out well for you or your relationship. If your partner seems reserved, the best thing that you can do to gain clarity is to ask them how they're feeling. It sounds simple because it is. The most direct answer that you're going to get is always going to come directly from them, not from your assumptions.

If your partner ever expresses to you that they do not wish to talk about something, respect this. It will show them that you're acknowledging their boundaries. A lot of couples feel that they're entitled to explanations from their significant others, but something that often gets overlooked is the establishment of boundaries. They are important and necessary.

When you can give your partner the space that they need, they will come to you when they're ready. Remember, they don't operate in the exact same way that you do. Give them time to open up and understand that it isn't always personal. They may just need a bit more time before they're ready to talk about their feelings. You don't need to blame yourself for any of this.

Let Go of the Past

We have all been hurt before, but that doesn't mean that the cycle needs to continue. If you let your past slip into your present, this is going to damage your marriage. The things that you've experienced with other people in other situations should no longer hold weight to your current relationship. This can become exhausting and upsetting if you continue to carry the baggage from past relationships. You deserve to live your life free of these burdens and healed from them. By recognizing the things that you're still holding on to, you can learn how to let them go in order to fully move on.

You might believe that you've already dealt with a situation, only to feel it come back to you in full force. The worst thing that you can do in moments like these is to blame your partner for what you're feeling. They were not responsible for this memory, so you need to learn how to separate the two. You must start by identifying why you're still being impacted by this particular situation. Consider how it has shaped you over the last few years.

Despite what you may be thinking, you don't need to ignore the past in order to move on from it. Doing the exact opposite in a productive way is how you'll make progress. Acknowledge what has happened to you and what you've been through. Think about how these situations and people have made you feel and recognize that these feelings are entirely valid. Now, think about how this all ties in with your current life and current relationship.

You are not the things that happen to you, but you are impacted by them. Consider the strengths that you've gained because of what you've gone through in your past. Realize how these experiences have helped shape you into the person that you are today. At the same time, realize that these are not the only things that make up who you are. You were born with a personality and traits that cannot be replaced. You are still you, regardless of what happens to you.

Work on gently letting go of thoughts about your past as they come to you. Remind yourself that they were once a part of your life, but now you're living a different chapter. This step doesn't happen overnight, but a healthy outlook on how to deal with your past can make a significant improvement in your relationship. When you can be focused on the present, you will be a lot more likely to put effort into your marriage and listen to what your partner is saying.

The following are some more tips that you can use to help you let go of your past and stay focused on your present:

- **Write Your Thoughts Down** - It can be helpful to say everything that you need to say on paper. You don't necessarily have to share your thoughts with anyone else, but it can be therapeutic to get them out. Once you've written them down, use this as a way to move forward. Tell yourself that these thoughts no longer need to come to your mind because you've already addressed them. You might have to do this several times before the habit sticks.

- **Keep Your Distance** - If you're trying to let go of memories that involve someone from your past, stay away from them in your present. Big problems can arise when you allow those from your past to linger. If you don't have a healthy relationship with this person, then there is no reason that you need to let them remain in your life. Do your best to distance yourself from them in order to protect yourself. Understand that you do not owe it to them to keep them close.

- **Accept a Lack of an Apology** - You aren't always going to get the "I'm sorry" that you desire. When you're dealing with a past situation that feels unresolved, you must create your own closure. Work with the issues that remain and think about ways that you can build yourself up instead of allowing these memories to drag you down. Know that you don't need to hear an apology in order to move on from someone or something. Find your inner strength.

- **Enjoy Love** - With your partner, you should be experiencing love in many ways. Allow them to make you feel important and cherished. When you are distracted, it can be easy to forget how much your partner does for you and how much they actually care. Learn how to set your sights back on this so that you can fully appreciate how much they love you.

- **Get Help** - If you're finding it difficult to let go of the past on your own, know that therapy is always an option. Talking to a professional can be a big help because this person is going to be someone that you don't already know and who won't have a biased opinion. Sometimes, you just need to talk to someone who is there to listen to you rather than give you advice. It can be very healthy for you to open up to a therapist as a way to begin addressing your past issues.

Develop Fun and Laughter

Being in a marriage that is full of laughter can really open up your abilities to love one another. Over time, arguments and disagreements can come between how you truly feel about one another. It can be very beneficial to get back to the basics of being able to just have fun together. Not only does this keep your relationship lighthearted, but it can also highlight certain things that you first noticed about your spouse as you were falling in love. It's no secret that the beginning of your relationship was probably simpler than it is right now. This is because of the newness that surrounded your love.

It is possible to get back to this carefree version of your love, as long as you're both willing to let go of the petty things. Understand what is actually worth holding on to and what doesn't actually matter. Certain arguments are going to be very temporary, but the anger and resentment can last for a long time. The sooner that you can let go of this negativity, the more fun that you'll begin to experience in your relationship. It can be like a refreshing boost of confidence that will show you exactly what unconditional love feels like.

Your marriage can be fun. Even despite all of the hard work that is involved, it's not impossible to bring back the laughter. Consider these tips for lightening the mood:

- **Keep Dating** - Once you're married, the concept of dating your significant other changes. You already have each other, so less effort needs to be made to win them over, right? Wrong. You should put in extra effort in order to show your partner exactly how you feel about them. One of the most fun parts of a relationship is the chase and just because you're already married doesn't mean that you need to stop this part. Keep flirting with your partner. It will bring back an exciting element to your marriage.
- **Put the Kids to Bed Early** - If you have kids, your life as a couple has shifted to cater to their

needs. Every once in a while, it's okay to put them to bed early in an effort to spend some alone time with your spouse. You both deserve this and it can do a lot for your marriage. It will likely take you both back to an earlier time in your relationship when the feelings were still fresh.

- **Sleep at the Same Time** - When you go to sleep, make sure that you're going to sleep at the same time as your partner. This will signify that you are both living your lives together, rather than being two people who live separate lives that share a bed. This dynamic can bring you a lot closer together as a couple. It will also establish a routine that can make you feel safe and secure. Plus, you will start each day on the same page. Allow your nights to be a time where you can talk freely and laugh as much as you want to. It's likely that you'll also sleep better when you are both resting your heads at the same time.

- **Send Risque Messages** - There is nothing more fun than receiving a risque surprise during your day. Keep your romance alive by spontaneously texting your partner. It's okay to be candid every once in a while, especially if you feel that you need to combat boredom as a couple. Know that these messages will keep your partner thinking about you until you're able to be together in person again. They can bring you closer and even reignite some of your passion.

- **Go on Dates That You Used to Go On** - Getting back to your old habits can bring back those old feelings of fun and excitement that you once had. Revisit restaurants and places that have a special meaning to you both. This will allow you to remember how it felt to fall in love with one another. You can also make new memories while you reminisce about the old ones.

- **Do Something Creative Together** - Creativity can bring out a lot of fun in any relationship. Work on a project together. It doesn't matter how experienced either of you is. A lot of the fun comes from learning together and experimenting with different ways to be creative. Couples who are able to work together in this way are typically able to turn frustrating moments into fun challenges.

- **Try Something New** - While a routine can be nice to have, it's also nice to break free from it every once in a while. Try something new together as a couple. This experience can give you a great chance to bond and see if you both share the same opinion on what you think about the new activity that you're trying. It prevents the relationship from becoming stale and allows you to develop new interests together as a couple.

Chapter 6:

What Trust Really Means

in Your Relationship

In any relationship, trust needs to be present in order to have a strong foundation. When you have all of the other components of a great relationship, such as romance and fun, this won't mean anything if you and your partner don't trust one another. Trust makes your relationship strong, and it allows you to get through anything together. Consider how strong this bond is. When you're able to fully love your partner, this likely means that you trust them. You can have trust before you have love, but you cannot have love without trust. When you realize how important one is to the other, you will be able to make it a priority in your marriage.

While there are many things that can get in the way of your trust, you should always try to find your way back to having a healthy level. Jealousy is one of the main reasons why couples might struggle with trust. There are many people who might find your partner attractive. This can understandably lead you to feeling insecure, especially if your partner does nothing to reassure you. When you have a healthy and trusting relationship, you shouldn't have to worry about your partner cheating on you. If you've already established that this is a terrible betrayal, your trust in your partner should tell you everything that you need to know. Other people might find them attractive or interesting, but they have chosen you.

If you've already established this with your partner, do your best to let go of your jealousy and insecurity. In a completely loyal relationship, couples can end up getting divorced because of the stress that jealousy brings. When you aren't able to let go of this complex, it can start to put a lot of pressure on your spouse and on your marriage. There's nothing worse than being accused of something that you aren't doing, even when you try to convince the person that you aren't guilty of it. This is why trust is so important. You should be able to take one another's word without having any feelings of doubt.

Why Trust Is Important

Without trust, you're missing the closeness that you should have with your partner. This is the person that you've chosen to spend your life with. You should be able to tell them anything and believe that they will always have your best interest at heart. Trust issues are very capable of tearing marriages apart. They can infiltrate your relationship and make it seem like there is nothing that you can do to fix it. When betrayal has already happened, this makes the trust especially hard to come by. You should always value trust in your relationship and you should do everything in your power to strengthen it.

Sharing trust in a relationship leads to many other great benefits. Trust can open the lines of honest communication. This means that you'll always be able to take what your partner says as the truth. You won't be left wondering if they're leaving out details or changing their words in an effort to mislead you. With a strong, trusting relationship, there is no need to believe that either one of you has a hidden agenda of any kind. It's a very freeing feeling to be able to openly trust your partner in any situation. You'll always know that you have someone on your side.

Life can be unpredictable, so it matters that you can have a partner that you feel comfortable relying on. Knowing that they're always going to be there to support you can be a great feeling, one that will motivate you to do better and to be better. This kind of mutual support is what creates a strong romantic foundation. As much as your partner is there for you, the same support can be reciprocated. Once you get into this habit, it becomes very easy to find ways to show your support and to encourage your partner in everything that they do. That way, they'll know that they also have someone who is on their side.

One of the biggest benefits of being with someone you trust is the lack of worry you'll face about them cheating on you. Those who constantly feel the need to check-in with their significant other to make sure they aren't being cheated on are likely not in the healthiest relationship. There should be nothing that your partner does that would make you think that they would be unfaithful. The bond of marriage is sacred in that it's only supposed to be shared by the partners who entered into it. When someone else comes between this bond, this creates a very big violation of trust that can be nearly impossible to recover from.

Through trusting one another, you will both get the chance to experience a certain degree of freedom. In the things that you say and do, you will both have clear understandings of what is acceptable and where the boundaries lie. This is why it's so important to let your partner know when they've done something that upsets you. Make it clear when you don't like a certain behavior in order to avoid being hurt again in the future. In turn, work to understand what your partner's boundaries are and respect them. When you can both be honest about your boundaries, there will be no confusion and no trust broken.

Intimacy is another factor in your relationship that is directly impacted by your level of trust. You're going to have difficulty being intimate with your partner if you don't trust them. In order to have sex with someone, you need a special bond and a certain type of attraction. Knowing that you share unlimited trust between the two of you can actually end up becoming a turn-on in your relationship. Use this to your advantage, allowing it to reignite the passion that you both feel for one another. You're also going to be able to become completely vulnerable to each other. This creates another positive element to your sex life by creating an erotic and an enticing mood.

Individually, the trust that you have in your relationship is also going to impact your self-esteem. You're going to feel like a much more confident person when you know that you can trust your partner. Without all of the worries that you would have to face if you didn't share this trust, you'll notice a wonderful sense of freedom and happiness that comes along with it. This confidence can allow you to reach for your goals and to try new things in life. It shows you that you can take opportunities and that you'll have a supportive partner who is going to be rooting for you the entire time. It also helps to know that they'll be there if anything goes wrong in life, comforting you and encouraging you to try again.

Cheating

Arguably the most severe betrayal, it can be incredibly hard to recover from being cheated on. This is an action that destroys trust and makes it difficult to rebuild. If you are experiencing a situation like this in your marriage, you are likely to feel a rollercoaster of emotions. Not only are you left to deal with the pain of being cheated on, but you must also make a very important decision regarding your marriage — are you going to work it out or are you going to leave?

No matter how much you want to rationalize it, you never should. Just because you love your partner does not mean that you need to put up with being treated poorly. You need to ask yourself if this is the relationship that you truly deserve. They need to jump into action, proving to you how they are going to make this up to you by winning back your trust. It can be a very complicated and difficult process. Understand that you call the shots here; you get to make the decision if you want to stay and work things out or if you'd rather move on with your life.

If you decide that you want to heal from this betrayal, know that you aren't the only one. So many couples go through this and end up realizing that their love is strong enough to last. It just takes a lot of hard work to regain the same level of trust you once had. After your partner has been unfaithful, it's likely that you're going to become very suspicious of their actions. Something that once seemed entirely normal, like going to the grocery store, can turn into a big series of what-ifs. You might be wondering if they're really going to the store or if they're going to meet up with someone else. This is a devastating reality to have to deal with.

Remember, if you were not unfaithful, this is not your problem to fix. Your partner needs to find their own ways to prove to you that they want to be with you. They need to establish that this relationship is more important than impulsive and hurtful decisions. Through their actions, they should be making an effort to re-establish the trust between the two of you. If you are doing all of the work, then the relationship still might not last. You don't need to fix something that you didn't break in the first place, but you do need to be aware of the way that you're being treated from now on.

Most couples need to get back to the root of their relationship, remembering how they ended up here in the first place. You need to fall in love with one another all over again, learning about each other's needs and desires. Your partner needs to make a major effort to prioritize you, proving that they want to be with you and only you. Given time, this is possible. You can return to the level of trust that you once had, but this is only going to happen if you both agree to fix the relationship.

A common problem comes when one person agrees to fix things, yet the other person doesn't think the issue can be solved in this way. Now more than ever, it's important that you're both on the same page. You each need to do what feels right individually and for the relationship, as well. This isn't something you can fix alone, nor should you need to. You're going to get your heart broken all over again if you think that you're on the path to fixing your marriage, yet your partner is not displaying the same level of commitment.

When you decide to forgive your partner for such an act, you need to remember that you are making a commitment too. By choosing to forgive them, you need to actively make sure that your actions are matching your words. While you are going to have a lot of built-up resentment, you need to do your best to work through this. Allow yourself to heal from the betrayal while taking care of your own emotional needs first. Couples therapy or individual therapy can be a great option for a situation like this. It can give you the chance to talk to someone with an unbiased opinion and help you work through your problems.

No one is going to know what you need to heal better than you. Once you figure this out, be vocal about it. Your partner should be eager to listen if they're serious about repairing the relationship. Don't feel selfish or guilty for having these requests because you deserve to feel secure in your marriage. Also, remember that your personal issues should stay personal. If you don't want to tell anyone about what has happened, your spouse should be able to respect this and also keep it to themselves. Your relationship issues are for the two of you to deal with, not the rest of the people in your lives.

Restoring Trust

- **Decide on Forgiveness** - When trust has been broken, this is an indication that someone has messed up. In some cases, both of you will be at fault. You need to ultimately decide that you are ready to forgive or to be forgiven. When you can both come to this conclusion, you will be ready to move on and heal your relationship. Staying stuck on the issue without coming to a resolution is very tiring and taxing. You don't deserve to stay in this negative headspace. Move on for the sake of your own well-being.

- **Discuss the Details** - Get all of the details about the betrayal that you need in order to fully understand it. Once you know the whole story, you'll be able to process the information and then move forward. When you're only hearing part of a story, this is going to skew your perception. Make sure you ask your spouse as many questions as necessary until you feel that you're both at this point.

- **Release Your Anger** - It's natural to feel anger, possibly at your partner and possibly even at yourself. Your feelings are valid and you need to have proper outlets for them. Make sure that you aren't holding these feelings inside because they'll begin to eat away at you. This also gives them the chance to appear again during the next confrontation that you have with your partner. Do everything you can for yourself to ensure that you have somewhere to release your negative feelings. Whether you take up a hobby or see a professional therapist, you need to be able to talk about these things openly before you can let them go.

- **Establish Your Desire** - Both of you should be able to express that you want the marriage to work. This is a part of being on the same page as a couple. No matter what you've gone through, the idea that you both want the relationship to work is a promising thought. It shows that you're both willing to do whatever it takes to allow the trust to flow again.

- **Be Open to Self-Improvement** - Sometimes, it takes a little bit of growth as an individual before you're able to grow as a couple. Be willing to do the things that you require until you're entirely happy with the person that you've become. Practice self-care frequently and listen to your own needs. These steps are important because it can be easy to lose sight of who you are as an individual rather than as your partner's spouse. Also, if both of you are willing to improve on yourselves, it makes it much easier to move past challenges in your relationship.

- **Be Aware of Your Feelings** - You are going to experience many different feelings while you're working on healing your marriage. Make sure that you take notice of all of them. They might be able to help you pinpoint exactly what you need in order to move forward. If you get a gut instinct, you should listen to it. These instincts can help you a lot when you're feeling conflicted about your relationship.

- **Shed Your Armor** - There is no need to place walls up with your partner, especially at a time like this. You need to work on staying open and communicating regularly. The conversations might be difficult, but it's a lot better to be honest than to be misled. Understand that this is what it's going to take in order to re-establish that sense of trust that you once shared. You don't need to put up a front; this is still your significant other, the person you once fell in love with.

- **Share Your Thoughts** - Work on making your voice heard at all times. If you have a thought that you feel needs to be expressed, don't hold back. This keeps the power balanced, ensuring that you're able to fully express yourself. If you allow yourself to be overshadowed by the problems that you're facing, there's going to be a lot more work to be done once you finally get over the problem at hand. Know that you are important, too.

- **Get Back to Basics** - Think about how you can restart your relationship. In a way, you're going to imagine that you're back to square one, first getting to know one another. You need to make sure that you're still compatible and that all can be forgiven. You need to have trust and loyalty, reassuring one another that you want this marriage to last.

Chapter 7

Trust — Essential and Fundamental to Any Relationship

Having a basic understanding of trust is great for your relationship, but you should know that trust is something to keep in mind at all times. You can always make an effort to build this trust and make sure that you're always being your best to your partner. This kind of devotion is essential for having a happy marriage. When you can understand that trust is a necessity, you're going to make it a part of your daily routine. Instead of being burdened by the idea of building trust with your partner, you'll begin to adopt and welcome these habits on a regular basis.

This chapter is going to focus on how you can be the happiest couple possible. You'll learn realistic ways to remedy your marriage and to develop healthy habits that will serve both you and your partner. Making a marriage last can definitely be hard work, but that is to be expected. It's one of the strongest bonds you'll ever know and it can evolve over time, just like people can. By remaining true to who you are, you'll be able to keep up with your own needs while also identifying your partner's needs. This ability to remain flexible is going to allow your marriage to feel rewarding and happy.

Remember that you both get to decide what a successful marriage looks like. Some couples value alone time while others value having a big family. You and your spouse don't have to follow any sort of standard. Just strive for the things that you both want and need to be happy. You'll know that you're successful when you feel that you're on the same page. Understand that trial and error is definitely going to be involved, no matter how long you've been together. This is the point of marriage — exploring and growing together while loving one another unconditionally. As cliche as it sounds, practice makes perfect. You need to practice your patience and your understanding in an effort to make your spouse feel heard. You'll also find that both of you need to work on your ability to compromise. With all of these things combined, you'll surely find a way to be happy together.

Staying True to You

It's important that you don't allow yourself to get lost while in a relationship. This tends to happen when you become so comfortable with being with your spouse that you forget to keep your own personal identity. The things that you're interested in and that are important to you matter. What makes you an individual is what made your partner fall in love with you in the first place. See if you can identify things that you enjoy without considering what your spouse thinks. This is a good test to see if you're still being true to yourself. Try to think only about yourself and your interests. This can be a very eye-opening experience for some.

If you have difficulty thinking about this, you might need to take some more time for yourself. There's nothing wrong with requiring a little bit of alone time every now and then. Your partner should understand that you deserve to do the things that you enjoy doing without impacting the love that you have for them. This isn't a personal attack on your partner but a way to make sure that you are still an individual. Most people don't realize that they've lost sight of who they are until it's too late. Getting into a fight with your partner and being forced to think and act on your own can be a way to realize that you don't exactly know who you are anymore.

When you're working on being true to yourself, consider the following tips:

- **Become Self-Serving** - Know that you can still fulfill your partner's needs while also taking care of your own. Do whatever you can for yourself. By knowing that you can take care of yourself and make yourself happy, anything your partner does for you will be extra. True happiness in a relationship starts with individual happiness. Neither one of you should have to rely on each other for your total happiness. When you can remember this, you'll feel more motivated to take action and to take care of yourself.

- **Share Your Thoughts** - As you become more comfortable with your partner over the years, it can become easier to just agree with them rather than expressing your own thoughts. This usually happens because couples tend to think alike as they grow closer. While this can be great in some ways, it's also one of the things that will rob you of your own identity. If you disagree with your partner, or if you have a differing opinion, make sure to let it be known. This will serve as a reminder to both yourself and your partner that you're an individual with a unique way of thinking.

- **Don't Always Aim to Please** - If you have a caregiver personality, it can seem natural to always want to please your partner. You might go out of your way to do things for them, just to make their life easier. This can be a kind gesture at times, but you need to remember to balance this out by taking care of yourself too. Know that you don't always have to aim to please them, especially when the situation involves both of you equally. When you can come together as a couple, you should both be able to put in the same amount of work. It becomes exhausting when you're always the one who is over-exerting yourself.

- **Live Through Your Values** - You should always be aware of the things that you value in life. They can shift over time, but they will always be present in your heart. Make sure that your actions align with these values and be sure to speak up if anything goes against them. By maintaining these values, you are being strong and staying true to yourself. No one else has to share the same values, but as long as they're important to you, then you need to make sure that you're upholding them. Make changes as necessary to ensure that you're living your life in the best way that you know how.

- **Trust Yourself** - This is a very big step to take in order to become the best version of yourself as an individual. While a lot of emphasis has been placed on having trust in your partner, you must also be able to trust yourself. Much like love, it's hard to trust someone when you don't even trust yourself. Do what you can to build up your self-esteem and prove to yourself why you know what is best for you. This process can be time-consuming, but it's going to be worth it. When you have this strong sense of trust in yourself, you will be able to feel confident about all of the decisions that you make.

- **Seek Growth** - Another downside of becoming very comfortable with your partner is the idea that you've reached a point where you no longer have to grow as an individual. It's understandable that your routines are your comfort zone, but you still need to step outside of them every now and then. Challenge yourself by putting yourself in situations that will encourage you to think outside the box. Do what you think is best for you and for your life at this moment. Ask yourself what you can change in order to promote even more self-growth.

When you value yourself, you're going to be able to value the actions that you take. Any decision that you make in your marriage will be justified and important. It's when you are feeling unsure of yourself that making decisions can seem very difficult. Use your confidence to your advantage and know that you understand your marriage best. While it's between yourself and your partner, only you know what your true feelings are.

In any relationship, there is an unconscious influence that impacts the actions that you take. This influence can come from past experiences in love, childhood upbringing, and more. Learn how to identify these things and know that they aren't always going to apply to your current situation. It can be hard to unravel these ideals because you won't always notice where you've seen them, but know that you can always create your own. Do what you really feel is best, not what your past experiences have shown you.

Placing naive trust in yourself is not the same thing as truly believing in yourself. If you can identify great qualities that you possess, you're going to be a lot more likely to experience a genuine kind of trust. Remind yourself of why you are a good person and what things you've already accomplished that are noteworthy. You might have to give yourself these reminders each day, but that is okay as long as they help you grow as an individual. As expected, the better you can trust yourself, the better the trust in your relationship will be.

How to Be Gentle and Patient

It takes a certain softness in order to be a gentle and patient spouse. When you're able to let your guard down and learn how to recognize when you're wrong, this is going to show your spouse that you care about their feelings. Nobody can always be right because this isn't realistic. There are going to be times when you have excellent points to make, but there will be other times when your ego might get the better of you. By working on ways to combat this selfishness, you're going to be a much better partner and this will lead to a happier marriage.

Seeing the good in your spouse is one of the most effective ways to foster this gentle side of yourself. When you can see where they're coming from and why they're doing what they're doing, you will likely be able to see many redeeming qualities. Know that not everything is a personal attack against you. If your spouse disagrees with an opinion that you have, maybe they believe in something else that matters to them. It's always better to assume the best in your partner rather than automatically jumping to the worst conclusion. This will inevitably lead to fights and disagreements. You don't need this kind of negativity in your life, so you should avoid it at all costs.

Slowing Down

Everyone can benefit from working on their patience. It can be tough to remain calm and patient when there is a lot going on around you. In a relationship, there is always going to be something that requires you to express your opinions or take action. It's a partnership, one that you must work together to maintain. Know that you don't have to quickly jump to making a decision, though. This is one way that you can practice your patience. By thinking carefully about your options when you can, you're going to be more likely to make a choice that you can feel proud of.

This is why it's essential that you think before you speak. Not every conversation will require you to quickly come up with a reply or a retort. By using your active listening skills, identify if the conversation needs a certain reply at all. Remember how valuable a keen listening ear can be. If your response is required, think carefully about how you feel and consider what's at stake. Remember to not only think about what your decision is going to do at the moment but how it will impact you in the future, as well. Considering your responses in this way allows you and your partner to communicate more effectively.

Cut yourself some slack and appreciate all that you do on a regular basis. While your spouse might already express gratitude for this, know that you should acknowledge your accomplishments too. Know that you don't always have to keep pushing for more and overextending yourself. This is going to lead you to feeling burnt out. Understand that your best is good enough and as long as you are giving the relationship your all, you don't have to push yourself past any limits that you have.

Eating Right

The food that you eat is going to make a huge difference in how patient you're able to stay. First of all, if you aren't eating enough, this is going to lead you to an automatic feeling of irritability. You shouldn't let yourself get to this point on a regular basis, and should instead aim to eat a healthy diet. Even if you feel that you aren't in a bad mood, your actions toward your partner might lead you to fight or argue. Be aware that you can come off a little intense when you're battling hunger.

Make sure that you fill up on foods that are actually providing you with nutrients. It can be easy to reach for junk food because it's a quick option, but eating junk food can be just as bad as not eating enough. Eat foods that are going to benefit the health of your brain and your body. These ingredients will fuel you and keep you going throughout your day. Some examples include fish, lean proteins, avocados, leafy greens, and other fruits and vegetables. If you find yourself getting randomly irritable throughout the day, you might need to make some changes in your eating habits.

Breathing

As mentioned, the way that you breathe is very important. It isn't going to be possible to stay patient when you are hyperventilating. Certain conversations might make your heart rate rise and your breathing rapid, but you need to learn how to become aware of this. When you're in this state of being, you're going to be more likely to snap at your partner or to say things that you don't mean out of anger. You need to find valid ways to calm yourself down in tense moments like these. Know that this is going to prevent a lot of difficulties in your relationship.

If you need to take a timeout, let your partner know. Certain conversations can be very taxing. Instead of forcing yourself through them, take a step back when need be. Make sure that you breathe in deeply and imagine yourself exhaling the negativity. It can be helpful to use a mantra such as the following:

"Inhale positivity; exhale negativity."

Recite something that applies to how you're currently feeling. If you need to come back to a conversation at a later time, remember to think carefully about how the first conversation made you feel. Do your best to enter the next one with a calm mindset and a steady heart rate. This is going to help you to remain calm and think rationally. If you feel yourself hyperventilating again, work on your breathing exercises.

In general, yoga can be a great form of exercise to practice because of its calming properties. It allows you to get some physical benefits while also teaching you healthy breathing practices that will clear your mind. Yoga helps you center yourself and is thought to make you a calmer person. When you can handle your temper, you'll feel a lot more confident in your ability to remain gentle and patient.

Doing a little bit of yoga before bed each night can prove to be very beneficial. It will allow you to empty your thoughts so you can start your day off right. Anything that promotes clear thinking is going to be especially valuable to you as you try to manage your anger. Everyone could use some practice with this, so don't feel like you're a bad person because of it. Set a clear focus on how you would like to use more patience and allow it to guide you throughout your day. Sometimes, just focusing your mind on something positive can be enough to change your entire outlook.

If you ever feel that you have gone beyond the point of no return with your anger, take the time to step back from the current situation that is stressing you out.

Breathe in through your nose for 7 full seconds and breathe out through your mouth for the same amount of time. This is going to get your heart rate back down. Know that this moment is going to pass and that you can return to your patience if you try hard enough. Tell yourself that when you go back into the situation, your outlook is going to be different. Remember, these things take practice so try to practice patience with yourself while you learn.

Chapter 8:

The Secret to Actions that

Will Grow Trust in Your

Relationship

Having a great marriage is all about taking actionable steps. It's only the beginning when you can both agree that your relationship needs work. The next part comes when you actually implement it. Like anything that you want to be successful at, you must come up with a plan. By agreeing on steps that you and your spouse can take together, you will both feel that you are making progress toward the end result — a happy marriage that is full of trust.

Think of changes that you can make that will improve your relationship in some way. You don't need to change everything just for the sake of making changes. Be smart about the decisions that you must make together. It's natural for couples to lose trust in one another over time, but your relationship doesn't need to stay this way. Much like love, trust can grow and it can also be lost. This is why it must be cultivated very carefully and paid attention to at all times. The instant that you stop monitoring the trust that you have, the more likely you are to become a spouse who is lazy and unaware of your partner's needs.

Consider that broken trust can come in many different forms. It doesn't necessarily have to stem from a betrayal or a deliberate action. This is why talking to one another openly is so important. A general rule is that if you feel hurt by your partner's actions, say something. What hurts you isn't always going to be apparent to them, so you need to bring it to their attention. Explain how you are feeling and try not to point any accusatory fingers. See what they have to say about your feelings and about how they can potentially correct their behavior. This is how you're going to enter an effective way to grow the trust that you have.

Make an Action Plan

Step 1: Identify why you're having trust issues. This doesn't need to be complicated or drawn out. Simply have an honest talk and discuss the things that stand out to you both. Even if you don't know why this is happening or how you're going to fix it, the very first step comes from being able to identify it. Don't be afraid to mention it if it is greatly impacting the way that you feel. Also, know that your spouse might have issues that are entirely different. Remember to respect one another and listen to both sides of the story. Allow your partner to completely finish talking before you launch into your own opinions.

If you're having trouble thinking about your trust issues, think back to the last time that you felt upset with your partner. What actions did they display that made you feel bad? This can be a very basic way to get into the topic of betrayal and mistrust. During this step, you aren't supposed to analyze anything or fix anything. The main objective is to state what the problem is so that you can both agree on a starting point for your action plan. It's more important than ever that you get on the same page from the very beginning. When you're both clear about what needs to be fixed, your solution is going to work well.

Step 2: Individually, talk about what you feel needs to change in the relationship. Know that this doesn't necessarily have to be the given solution, but hearing this input can help you both by shedding more light on the situation. This part might require some time to think. If you need to each have some space in order to come up with the answers, allow this to happen. Know that you don't need to rush during any part of this plan. Careful thought is going to create better results. As you know, thinking hard before you speak will lead you to your most honest feelings.

Again, let one another fully complete their thoughts before jumping in. When you can communicate without interrupting each other, you will both feel that you had equal time to express your opinions. This is going to avoid any additional conflicts or fighting. Know that talking about sensitive subjects isn't easy, but it must be done in order to truly get to the bottom of things. You might get emotional, but that is okay. It's a sign that you care about fixing the problem. Don't be afraid to wear your heart on your sleeve. This is the step where you'll need to practice vulnerability. Know that your partner isn't listening to judge you. The reason why you're both having this conversation should be clear by now — you want to fix things.

Step 3: Work on healing. This is going to be a diverse step because it can involve a number of different strategies. When dealing with broken trust, this an indication that you have something to heal from. Whether you need to do this alone or with your partner, now is the time to identify what it's going to take to make you feel better. If you don't know, start from within. Work on yourself in order to become the best version of you that you can possibly be. Incorporate various self-care tasks into your daily routine as a reminder that you matter. As you know, it becomes hard to think about yourself when you're devoted to being a great partner.

If the healing process requires that you both work together, make a commitment to work on this on a regular basis. You can't expect to talk about it one time and for the feelings to disappear. This is going to be a process. Tell your partner if there is anything that they can do to solidify the trust. This isn't going to be a one-sided endeavor. Know that you might also be required to work on certain behaviors or habits that are hindering the relationship. Being stubborn during this step is only going to set you both back. You must be willing to hear this constructive criticism about yourself if you want to see an improvement in your marriage.

Step 4: Brainstorm together. This step is probably going to take the most work out of all of them, but it's helpful because it encourages you to think about the problem together instead of nit-picking it individually. Now is the time to drop any ill feelings about the issue. If you feel that you still need time to heal, then you need to stay on the previous step for as long as it takes to move forward from the issue. Again, there is no set timeline on how long you need to spend on each step. You can take as long as you personally feel that you need. The more thorough that you are, the less likely that the problem is just going to return again in the near future. Many couples make the mistake of thinking that they've solved their problem, yet they've only skimmed the surface.

You need to think deeply about the issue, considering all possible solutions. Don't rule anything out because your solution might be something that you have yet to try. When you make assumptions and remove information from your brainstorming session, you're giving the relationship less of a chance. Understand that the more detailed you are, the more effectively you will be able to find the solution that works best for both of you. Writing down all of your options can be helpful. It will allow you both to keep track of what can be done.

Step 5: Follow through with the solution. It's only one part of moving on to identify what you are going to do. Then, you must put the "action" in your action plan. Take the necessary steps to make the solution your new reality. Make sure that you verbally discuss what these steps are so you can hold each other accountable for upholding them. If you know exactly what needs to be done, there will no longer be confusion surrounding the issue. This part can be a little bit challenging, but it should be clear enough for you to have a guided path. Follow the steps and you won't go wrong.

Give this solution time. Know that your problems aren't going to get better overnight. It can take days, or weeks, to fully implement them. Don't be so quick to give up. If you have gone several months, however, without any changes, then it might be a good idea to go back to the previous step. From here, you can revisit your other solutions to see if one of them is going to work out better. This is also why it's so helpful to have them written down as a reference sheet for you to look back on. Keep doing this until you both feel that you've found a solution that is yielding results. You should be able to identify if it's working if you feel that you are trusting one another more and getting along better.

Come to an Agreement

There are many instances in which you and your spouse will need to reach an agreement. Trust issues are only a part of this practice. There are other ways that the two of you will need to come together in order to achieve a happy and harmonious marriage. An example comes from the way that you run the household. From the very basic actions of doing the dishes to washing the laundry, you'll both need to agree on how you'd like to accomplish these chores. Believe it or not, when you aren't on the same page for the minor things, this can lead to major issues. At the root of the decisions that you make together, understand that a little bit of communication can go a long way.

When you treat one another with love and respect, these small things won't seem like a big deal when you need to discuss them. It's easy to feel the need to take your anger out on someone when other things in your life become stressful, especially the person who you know is supposed to love you unconditionally. You need to avoid this by managing your own feelings. If you're stressed out and it has nothing to do with your significant other, you need to take some time for yourself to figure out how to de-stress. This will keep you from blowing the little things out of proportion. In turn, your partner should treat you with the same level of respect.

Don't go off on one another the instant that you're hit with intense feelings. The idea behind dealing with your feelings on your own means that you'll be able to control your temper. Anger is a big reason why fights start. This anger can quickly evolve into words that you wish you could take back. Before you get to this point, think about what is actually making you angry. If your partner has nothing to do with it, consider going to them for a different reason — venting. If you need to talk about your anger, this is perfectly fine. Your spouse will be willing to listen and it will be a lot healthier to discuss it in this way instead of unintentionally blaming them for the way you feel.

Create opportunities for the two of you to work together instead of focusing on the things that you do differently. Marriage is about compromise, so it can be beneficial to learn directly from the source. See what your spouse can teach you and what you can provide them in return. By coming to an agreement that you will work on things together, this also requires you to focus on the partnership element of your relationship. It will highlight the things that you do well together and it will show you what you need to work on. Both are great and will encourage growth within your marriage.

Nobody likes to focus on the mistakes they've made, but having a sense of understanding when you do make a mistake is important. Not only will it show you what you did wrong, but it will allow you to work on making things better in the future. By turning a blind eye to your mistakes, this is only going to show your partner that you don't want to make any improvements. When you're in a marriage, your actions impact your partner almost as much as they impact yourself. You need to take this into consideration the next time that you feel stubborn or unwilling to change. Growth is a positive thing, both for yourself and for your relationship.

When you come to a certain agreement, it can help to write this down. This will place importance on the issue that you're trying to fix. No matter how big or small it is, both of you should sign this agreement so that you can acknowledge what the problem is and how you're going to fix it. This will serve as both a reminder and motivation for the future. Doing things this way can be unconventional, but it can help provide structure in your marriage. A lot of couples need the reintroduction of structure in order to get better at it and there is nothing wrong with that. Try it out for yourself and see if it makes a difference.

Know that situations change. This is why it's important to review anything that you've agreed upon every so often. If something changes, then it's justifiable that you would have to come together again to think of a new agreement. This is how you're going to practice working together and making successful decisions. As much as your partnership is romantic, it should also be practical. Couples who get along well understand that there are times when they need to be more relaxed and times when they should practice being serious. The more that you work together with your partner, the better you will be at identifying when you need to change the mood.

Overall, being able to agree on things comes down to how much effort you and your partner put into your marriage. If you just sit back and accept what is happening, then you aren't taking much accountability for your actions. You must stay engaged if you want your partner to know that you still care.

How to Engage in Your Marriage

- **Ask Questions** - Instead of assuming how your spouse feels because you already know them very well, ask them how they feel. This is important to stay engaged in the relationship because you should know that their feelings can change. Just as you will evolve as a person, so will they. Make sure that you continue to show an interest in knowing who they are right now, not just who they were when you first met.

- **Spend Time in New Situations** - Experiencing something new together is a great way to even the playing field. Since neither one of you will know exactly what to expect, you can enjoy this bonding experience as a way to work together and to discuss how you're feeling. This can be something simple like going to a new place or going on a double date with another couple. Alternatively, it could be something more complicated like planning a trip together or taking up a new hobby.

- **Put the Phone Down** - When you talk to your spouse, don't be distracted. Being comfortable around one another is a great thing, but not when you're sacrificing your significant other's feelings, this defeats the purpose. Make eye contact and put your phone down. Have a genuine conversation where you can truly connect without the need for any absentminded distractions.

- **Do Something They Enjoy** - There are going to be plenty of things that your spouse likes to do that you are less familiar with. For a change, engage in an activity or hobby that your spouse enjoys. If possible, let them teach you about it or guide you through it. This is a great way to change the relationship dynamic and the routine without the need to do anything complicated.

Chapter 9:

How to Regain Trust in a

Relationship That Is

Falling Apart

You aren't the only person in a marriage to feel that your relationship is falling apart — many feel that their relationships are broken beyond repair. This chapter asks you to be honest with yourself and to decide on how much your relationship matters to you. If you are willing to fix it and implement the changes, you will be able to give your marriage a fighting chance. All things fall apart at times, but that doesn't mean that you have to live this way. This can bring forward a lot of negative energy, causing you to fall into a downward spiral. No one deserves to live this way and you're going to learn how to break free of these chain reactions.

Starting by getting rid of the idea that you are helpless, you are going to find your inner-strength and recognize what needs to be done in order to fix your marriage. You will be able to effectively communicate these issues to your spouse in an effort to shed some light on what you've been dealing with. In discussing these things, you might be surprised to find that your spouse can identify with you. Making discoveries like this one will bring you closer together. It will serve as a reminder that you are not alone in this and that any relationship is made up of the actions of two people combined.

When you're able to move past making excuses, you're going to see real progress. The passion that you once shared will be reignited and you will both be happier than you've felt in a long time. Getting stuck is natural for all couples. Because no one is exempt, it can often feel as though you are trapped. In order to get out of this mentality, you need to remind yourself of all the freedoms that you still have. From the freedom to make changes in your life to the ability to work on yourself as an individual, there is always more that you can do to help improve the health of your marriage and to regain the trust that you once had.

Recognize Emotional Disconnect

If you feel that your partner is being distant with you, this could indicate that there is some emotional disconnect occurring. You might notice that your partner is pulling away, both figuratively and literally. This can naturally cause you to become very upset, possibly even accusatory at your partner's actions. There is a lot that can lead to emotional disconnect, so it's important that you recognize the signs so that you can talk to your partner about it in the best way possible. This will allow the two of you to have an honest conversation and to help strengthen your trust in one another.

- **Lack of Conversation/Shared Feelings** - One main sign of your partner pulling away might be their lack of interest in talking to you. They're likely doing so to avoid conversations that might have to do with their feelings or problems. If they used to talk to you about these things before, their behavior is going to be very noticeable. When you try to ask them what's wrong, they might change the subject or just lash out at you to avoid getting into a discussion. Naturally, this can be very painful for you to discover because it's going to be apparent that the trust you once shared is no longer present.
- **Distant Behavior** - When you do get the chance to talk to your partner, you might notice

that they seem distant or distracted. You might be telling them all of your feelings and yet they only give you short answers or try to change the subject. This is definitely a sign of emotional disconnect and it might be stemming from their inability to connect with the conversation that you're presenting to them. It can be very frustrating, especially when you feel that you are giving it your all. As you know, it takes two people to be in a healthy relationship. If one person is putting in all of the effort, this will create an imbalance.

- **Blind to Emotions** - If you express your emotions with sadness, rage, or even tears, this might still not be enough to elicit a response from your partner. Whether they're unaware of your emotions or ignoring them, they're likely not going to respond to you or ask you what's wrong. This can often be a coping mechanism for when situations get emotionally intense. By keeping themselves distanced, they won't have to launch into the discussion with you. This behavior will end up making you feel that they don't care at all. In reality, they might just not know how to cope with what is going on and thus be trying to avoid the situation.

- **No Conflict Resolution** - Your partner will begin to show a lack of interest in resolving any conflicts that you get into. When a fight occurs, they will likely find a way out of it or simply express that they don't want to discuss it any further. You might notice that they even seem indifferent when something is impacting you or your relationship. Frustration is probably going to be one-sided because your feelings will be hurt and they will keep going as if nothing is wrong. It can seem difficult to get through to your partner on any level, even if there is a big issue that is hindering your relationship.

- **No Quality Time** - Part of being in a relationship means that you and your partner should have quality time together. This is your chance to regroup and hear what is on each other's minds. If your partner stops showing interest in being alone with you or keeps changing the plans so that other people are involved, this can be an indication that they're feeling emotionally disconnected. The thought of this might make them uncomfortable or nervous, causing them to find ways to change the situation so there is little chance that you'll have to talk about their behavior. They might even go as far as pretending that they have other plans or that they're too busy doing something else.

- **Non-Existent Sex Life** - Having sex is one of the most emotional acts that a couple can engage in together. If your partner isn't connecting with you emotionally, the sex is likely to become sparse or stop altogether. If intimacy becomes an issue like this, bringing it up to your partner is probably only going to cause a fight or be met with excuses. In some cases, your partner might even blame you or something that you've done for their lack of sexual interest. This is something that can hinder couples very easily. It can cause insecurity and, sometimes, resentment. You will notice that you'll start to feel uncomfortable when the idea of having sex with your partner comes to mind.

Drop the Excuses

In relationships, it becomes very easy to fall into certain habits. When you get into conflicts with your spouse, it can be easier to just say what they want to hear or give them an excuse in order to prevent the situation from escalating. What you must be mindful of is the fact that this will not fix the problem. It's simply going to delay it until it comes up again in the future. Making an excuse for something that is wrong is not a valid way to resolve it. While it might seem like it fixes things, for the time being, it's likely to come back as an even bigger issue later on. Be aware of this habit and recognize if you do this.

If you want your partner to fully trust you, then you need to show them that you aren't just going to come up with an excuse when you hurt them or betray them. Issues should be discussed when they're fresh on your mind. This will allow you to fully tap into the emotions that you're feeling. Together as a unit, the two of you should be able to work things out. When your partner displays this kind of behavior, let them know. Without blaming them for any of the issues that you're having, try to bring it to their attention when they're telling you excuses instead of explaining how they really feel. This can potentially open up a new dialogue. While it might be hard to have conversations like these, they are necessary.

Open yourself to the idea that you might be wrong about something. A lot of people have a fear of being wrong and this is one way that excuses tend to appear. Know that you aren't perfect and your spouse knows that, too. They love you for who you are. It's a very humbling experience to realize that you've gotten something wrong, but you can learn a lot from it. Try your best to be open to these instances. When you do not have an answer for something, be honest with your partner instead of trying to make one up. This is going to further humble you and encourage you to be completely honest instead of hiding behind your mistakes with excuses.

Allow yourself to apologize to your partner if you do find that you've made a mistake. Honest mistakes require honest apologies. It will show them that you care about hurting their feelings or lying to them, two very big factors of any relationship. The more that you are honest with them, the more you'll be able to be honest with yourself. If you do have to apologize for something that you've done, consider this a new starting point. Once you've made amends, you can try again and be better. You don't need to punish yourself or prevent yourself from speaking up again in the future, just learn from the experience and move on.

Try not to compare yourself to other people. You are who you are, and you should be proud of that. Again, your partner is with you because of this, not because you're a copy of someone else. It can be easy to make excuses when you're trying to fit a certain mold. You might have to focus on some self-love in order to get back to what is important. Understand what qualities you have to offer and what you bring to the relationship. Give yourself credit for all that you've accomplished. You shouldn't have to change who you are to make your marriage work, but small efforts of self-improvement will be noticeable.

Make sure that you remain realistic during any discussions that you have with your partner. If you're expecting them to drop their way of thinking to adopt your own, you're going to be met with frustration. Understand that they are going to have their own process of working through issues and that you need to respect it. Not being able to think the exact same way shouldn't be an excuse that is used as to why conflict cannot be handled. You should still be able to come together as a couple to identify what actually can be changed and what will improve the situation.

Don't blame other people for your own actions. This is another common excuse that is made, and it allows you to get out of taking accountability for the things that you've done. Just because another person might have influenced you doesn't mean that they forced you to act the way that you did. All of your actions were chosen because you made the decision to implement them. It's important that you always keep this in mind, even if you mess up badly. Instead of making excuses for what you've done, you need to come up with ways to fix the situation and prevent yourself from making the same choices again in the future.

Identify Chain Reactions

When your decisions activate a chain of results, this is what is known as a chain reaction. Some people might refer to it as a domino effect. You need to be aware of these reactions in your relationship, as they can tell you a lot about why you have trust issues and what is holding you back as a couple. A chain reaction can be either positive or negative. If you can eliminate the negative chain reactions by avoiding what triggers them and strive for more positive ones, you'll notice a significant improvement in your relationship. The only way for you to do this is by being aware of these cycles and what behaviors set them off.

Positive

Some examples of positive chain reactions include:
- Regular laughter together
- The ability to be relaxed/happy
- Feeling close to one another

- Enjoying one another's company
- Understanding that trust and confidence is your foundation
- Feeling respected and heard
- A sense of attraction present
- Love flowing on a daily basis
- A noticeable desire for one another

Negative

Some examples of negative chain reactions include:

- Anger experienced on a regular basis
- A built-up feeling of resentment
- Blaming one another for issues
- Not respecting boundaries
- Feeling personally attacked
- Distance being present
- Talk of breaking up happening frequently
- Feeling jealous/insecure
- One person losing interest in the relationship
- Feeling that the marriage is falling apart

Given the above examples, you should be able to identify if any of these things are present in your current situation. A chain reaction is something that usually cannot be stopped once it is started, this is why it's important to identify it at the source. Take a look at which behaviors lead to bigger issues or greater benefits. This is how you'll be able to tell what to eliminate and what to do more of in your marriage. For this step, it's going to take some attention to detail as well as some patience.

Work on rebuilding your trust by letting your partner know that you want to eliminate negative chain reactions. When you can explain that both of you are going to have work together to accomplish this goal, this will make it less of an attack and more of a process. With both of you paying attention to what triggers these reactions, you should be able to come together and find a way to operate in your marriage without causing anything so extreme. Know that you can stop this series of reactions if you put in the effort to do so. By allowing your partner to know what you'd like the goal to be, they'll have a clear understanding of how much the relationship means to you.

If one of you seems to always be the cause of these chain reactions, this should become apparent once you start observing them. Pay attention to how each of you reacts when something bad is happening to you both. Know that your actions might be fueling the fire. If you're doing something that is causing a reaction and either you notice it or your partner points it out, you'll be able to know when to stop and think of ways to fix it. If you notice that your partner is at-fault, bring the issue up with them. Instead of trying to correct it, allow them to come up with their own way of doing so. This will show them that you aren't trying to control or nit-pick them but simply attempting to improve the quality of the relationship.

When you're both acting on your best characteristics, you're going to feel like the relationship has entered into a new chapter. You will both likely feel refreshed and able to handle whatever comes your way. It's amazing how tiring it can be to constantly have to deal with the same problems repeatedly, especially if these problems tend to lead to stressful arguments. Showing your best characteristics encourages you to live your life with your best foot forward. It will allow you to think about the smartest decisions that will ultimately lead you to the most harmony possible within the marriage.

Make sure that you're always as approachable as possible when your partner tries to come to you with a problem that they would like to fix. If you are truly on the same team, you'll be willing to work with them to improve the relationship. An unwillingness to talk comes across as standoffish. This can create fights as well as chip away at the trust that you have already built up together. In any relationship, there is going to be a time when you must do away with your complaints and simply handle what is going on. You'll be glad you did, and your partner will see that they don't have to work on things alone.

Chapter 10:

The Long-Term Benefits of Rebuilding Lost Trust in Your Relationship

The work that you put into your relationship does not only help at the moment but in the future as well. All of the efforts that you put into your marriage right now will carry over into your future interactions. This means that you aren't only solving problems and dealing with current issues together, but you're also learning how to practice longevity. All couples strive for longevity in their marriages. Because you want to be with your partner for the rest of your life, you need to understand that everything that you do right now is going to make a difference in your relationship. Be cautious about what you say and do in times of anger or stress. These things that might seem insignificant right now can become magnified over time, leading to fractures within the bond you share.

As you work through this guide together, you are both making a commitment to the overall health of your marriage. You are stating that you believe in the relationship and that you see it working out in the long-run. Those who have to question their significant others about whether they still want to be together will likely not be going through these exercises together. Know that if your spouse is willing to make changes and improvements, they are likely to believe that the love *is* going to make it and that the relationship *will* last. You need to have faith in one another as you explore this together. Rebuild your trust and enjoy the newfound connection that you discover.

Re-Establishing Your Connection

1. **Make your intentions clear.** This is a way for you to be extremely genuine with your spouse. Even if you do not align on certain ideas, if you

both have the same intentions behind your actions, you are going to be met with results that both of you are happy with. Oftentimes, couples will try to make this more complicated than it really is. You don't need to adjust your ideals to the point that they're identical, just get them moving in the same direction.

2. **Understand that love is powerful.** While a relationship is built on a lot more than the love that you share, it's still a very powerful element of any marriage. Use this love wisely and allow it to guide you when you are at a loss for what to do. This connection is one of the most genuine aspects of the relationship that you share. It was there in the beginning and it should continue to remain present until the very end. This is a constant that you can rely on.

3. **Agree to disagree sometimes.** You should know that not all arguments or conflicts need to be held in the same regard. Some are going to be pointless and you both need to recognize these limits. If you can just agree to disagree and then move on, this is a very healthy practice to learn as a couple. In doing so, this is going to save you a lot of time and effort while also allowing you both to potentially look back and laugh about this issue. It is a way that you can make your connection strong by realizing that you both don't need something like this in your life.

4. **Choose honesty over a white lie.** While telling a small lie to your partner might seem harmless, know that it's always going to get back to them. If you lie with the intention of making them feel better, you're doing a lot more than you need to be doing. It is easier to just express how you really feel and deal with it instantly rather than letting something go on for an extended period of time. Also, being honest with them keeps them in the loop. There is no worse feeling than being the last to find out about something, especially relating to your marriage, so remember to be honest with each other.

5. **Brainstorm together frequently.** Even if you aren't fighting and looking for a solution, it's a great idea to continually brainstorm with your significant other. You can discuss ideas and opinions this way. It provides you with a great outlet for your thoughts while also encouraging you both to make the best decisions that will benefit the overall health of the relationship. Use these brainstorming sessions to learn new things about one another. You can also use them to help each other figure out how to achieve your goals as individuals and as a couple.

6. **Allow yourself to let go of control.** There will be times when you really don't want to let go of being right. This is a form of control that you need to be aware of. It shows your partner that

you trust them when you are able to step away from something that you believe in because you see value in their approach, as well. This becomes a great way for you to show that you're able to compromise and stick with decisions that aren't always your own. Every couple should be able to reach this point together if they want a sense of balance in their relationship.

7. **Give a sincere apology when you need to.** Stepping down when you have done something wrong can be incredibly difficult, but it's time to swallow your pride. Give a heartfelt apology to your partner when you need to say that you're sorry. Don't do it because you have to or because you feel that you should. This will only come off as ingenuine. The words should come from your heart and the timing should make sense based on what is currently going on. These things matter if you want to have a thriving marriage that is full of trust.

8. **Know not to push certain buttons.** You know your partner better than anyone else and this means that you definitely know what tests their limits. It can be tempting to push them close to their boundaries without crossing any lines, but this is known as button-pushing. It's a negative action because it's normally done in a deliberate fashion. Don't allow yourself to take things to this point. You need to exercise your own form

of self-control in order to avoid pushing your partner's buttons. This is a sign of respect and of how you value your partner.

9. **Always think positively.** No matter what is going on in your life or in your marriage, you need to set your sights on positivity. If you get too caught up on what is negative, it's going to be difficult for you to move forward. Envision the positive results that you're hoping for and your actions will begin to align with your efforts. There is no use in tormenting yourself by replaying the negative possibilities over and over again in your head.

10. **Enforce your boundaries.** While you might not want to remind your spouse of the things that you aren't okay with, it becomes necessary to do so if your boundaries aren't being respected. In the same way, you shouldn't feel offended if they remind you of their own. Boundaries are important for every couple to have, regardless of how long they've been together. Your boundaries are a set of your own personal beliefs that matter to you. If your spouse truly loves you, they should have no problem respecting these boundaries and being sure to listen to you when any lines have been crossed. You should also be able to do the same for them without taking the request as a personal attack.

What You Will Learn

- Instead of coming up with ways to pick apart flaws and point out weaknesses, you will learn how to accept these things about your spouse.
- Holding on to resentment/bitterness is only going to end up hurting you after a while. You will learn how to let go of it and to move on from it.
- The focus will shift to the qualities that you can appreciate most about each other instead of the qualities that could use some improvement. Being able to acknowledge these things will allow you to pay your spouse better compliments.
- Talking about hardship or difficulty doesn't always have to result in a fight. As a mature couple, you should be able to get into these discussions and talk about these things honestly.
- The longer that you work toward overcoming your differences, the shorter your fights will last. Once you get into a method that works well for both of you, this process is going to become easier.
- Instead of keeping your distance when things get hard, you will learn to come together and begin working on your issues immediately. There is nothing worse than allowing separation

to overtake your relationship, causing emotional distancing.

- On a daily basis, you should be able to do things for one another that show you truly care. These things should be unprompted and done because of the love that you share.

- When healing is necessary, you will both be able to rely on constructive methods of getting to this point instead of continually resorting to behavior that ends up hurting you or the relationship.

- Reframing your approach can be beneficial when you're trying to solve problems. Instead of jumping straight into possible solutions, you will learn how to see things from new perspectives to see if it helps make things easier.

- Issues in the past can stay in the past if you move on from them properly. There shouldn't be anything residual that you're holding on to that is hindering your marriage today.

- When you see negativity, you will start with the attitude that you do not wish to carry it with you. After having this in your mind, you will be a lot more likely to find a solution for it rather than starting fights over it.

- You will learn how to enjoy what feels like a new life with your significant other. It can be a very refreshing feeling to realize that you do not have to be controlled by your trust issues and your problems.

- Couples should also be friends. When you can have a genuine friendship with your spouse, this is going to make your bond even stronger and show you different sides of each other.
- The two of you should be able to come to an agreement of what your "dream relationship" looks like. This kind of vision should come from how you wish your relationship could be in an ideal world. Together, you can strive to make this a reality.

This is only the beginning of what you will learn as you work through this guide. All of these examples can serve as motivation for you to use moving forward. A part of changing your behavior is changing your mindset. When you have the above examples to think about, you should be able to let go of any negativity that you might still be holding on to. Think deeply about why you might still feel the need to hold on to it, then let go of it in the best way that you know how. Understand that you don't need to remain in a state of worry or anxiety if you can personally clear your head enough to focus on the positive things about your marriage. If any issues come up, trust that your spouse will make them known and then you can work on solving them together.

Long-Term vs. Short-Term

When thinking about their problems, couples usually make the mistake of only considering what is going on in the present moment. Think back on the things that frustrated you the most last year. Do these things matter as much to you this year? Do you even remember what they are? Your mood has a lot to do with your reactionary impulses and you cannot necessarily help that. If something bothers you, then you're going to react to it — it's that simple. What you can do, however, is to learn how to think about the bigger picture. Understand that what might be bothering you right now might prove to be insignificant in the future.

When defining "the future," know that this can be anywhere from years later to weeks later. You need to consider if any issue is important enough to hold on to and if it will impact you in the future. If the issue is very temporary, meaning that it is likely to be resolved quickly, this is something that you shouldn't need to hold on to and take with you into the future. It is only going to take up negative space in your brain and hold you back from being the best partner that you can be.

For more serious and ongoing issues, you might need to carry them for a little while. This still does not warrant carrying them in a way that places weight onto your relationship. Know that the only reason problems need to go unresolved is if they need additional time to fix. For example, it might take time to rebuild trust once it has been broken. For anything that has a clear solution, do your best to consider it as handled. This way, you won't feel the need to bring it up again unnecessarily or use it against your partner in the future.

You will feel a lot better when your conscience is free of these things that simply take up space.

Consider this example:

You and your spouse have been fighting a lot over the amount of time that is spent going out with friends rather than the amount of time that is spent with each other. It has been causing fights that come to the same conclusion — you want your partner to stop going out. This has then caused a negative chain reaction and your spouse has become emotionally distant, avoiding you and avoiding having this conversation again. They continue to go out with friends and it continues to make you upset. There is no resolution.

Short-term solution: You don't talk to your partner until they stop going out as much. This causes a lot of tension in the relationship and the issue often gets brought up in fights, even when they have nothing to do with this subject. Your partner develops a defensive type of aggression that tends to come out when you nit-pick at them for going out. The cycle repeats itself until you both feel exhausted. You both keep doing it because it seems easier than addressing the issue and working on finding a solution that you feel would benefit you both.

Long-term solution: You both sit down and talk about the issue, expressing both sides of the story. Your partner wants to feel that they have their own individual life, but you don't want them gone late into the night. You come to a compromise, showing one another that you both value your marriage. Instead of going out all the time, your partner has their friends come over. This no longer makes you mad because your boundaries are respected. With this solution, you both feel that the issue has been taken care of, therefore, you don't continue to bring it up again in the future.

As you can see, each solution would result in very different outcomes. When you think that you are "handling" a problem, you might realize that you're only coming up with a temporary and short-term solution. Recognize these instances and see how you can change them for the better. Adjust what you're doing so that you can make them long-term, instead. The latter is going to leave you feeling a lot better about the solution and it will encourage you both to speak up about what you feel should be done.

Passive-aggressive techniques should not be used, as they are solely meant to make the other person feel bad. Remember, you need to always make sure that you are acting out of love. No matter what the situation is, that love for your partner should not simply disappear. Allow it to guide you and provide you with a new way of thinking. Understand that you aren't always going to get exactly what you want, but there are ways to come up with a compromise that will leave you feeling just as satisfied. It's all about being willing to work with one another. Long-term solutions leave you with long-term results. You know how frustrating it can be to repeat the same cycles, so do everything that you can to avoid this from the beginning.

Conclusion

This guide has given you valuable resources that you can now use to identify any problems that you are having, heal from the things that have hurt you in the past, understand why you have the habits that you do in your relationship, and work together as a couple to come up with the best solutions. It serves as a comprehensive look at exactly what it takes to be happy in your marriage. All of these tips and exercises stem from real ways that couples communicate and interact with one another in healthy relationships. Both of you should feel that you're being equally respected while being treated with care. The happiness that you're able to work toward together is not going anywhere, as long as you are both on board with the process.

After exploring all of the new ways that you can improve your marriage, you should be feeling inspired and proactive. Any relationship can be hard work, but the promise of being together forever brings forward a different kind of pressure. Understand that you are both going to change as individuals and this will, in turn, impact your relationship. You do not need to lose trust or betray each other in the process, though. Your ability to remain flexible to changes and your willingness to think outside of the box is going to greatly benefit both of you as you aim to rebuild your trust in the relationship.

Aim to understand your spouse and do your best to listen attentively to their needs. You don't need to rush this process because it sends them the message that you don't care about how they are feeling or what they are thinking. After taking their side into consideration, you should be able to come up with solutions together on how you want to fix your problems. In any harmonious marriage, this part needs to be balanced. This means that you both need to come up with solutions and agree on one together. When you're both putting in the same amount of work, fewer problems are likely to surface as a result.

Stop with the excuses and the avoidance that you have when you encounter problems. The best way to handle any issue in your relationship is going to be addressing it head-on. If you wait until it upsets you to the point of breaking, then you're likely going to lash out at your partner which will cause even more damage. Talking openly and honestly can be difficult, but it is necessary. Your communication is a direct way to identify if your marriage is healthy or not. You should be able to talk to one another about anything at any time without holding back or feeling judged. Make sure that you are doing your part to keep this communication flowing.

By choosing to take deliberate action, you will start to notice significant improvements in the way that you get along and are able to keep your happiness flowing. Not only will your efforts be beneficial when you're working through problems, but they will also set a strong foundation for the future. Your significant other should be a priority to you, so you should let them know by allowing your actions to match your words. Do kind things for them and remember to consider their love language. At the end of the day, you should both feel appreciative of one another and lucky to be in the relationship that you are in.

As promised, you were given all of the tools that you need to move forward in your marriage. Instead of getting caught up in past issues and the same problems, you will be able to make decisions that are going to benefit the health of your relationship. Your marriage is going to feel stronger and happier, allowing you to feel that you can be yourself without any consequences. The best marriages are a true partnership with a sense of freedom that is still present. You should do things together because you want to, not because you feel that you have to. The love that you share should shine through any difficulties that you encounter because it is going to be stronger than ever.

Do not go yet; One last thing to do...

If you enjoyed this book or found it useful I'd be very grateful if you'd post a short review on Amazon.com. Your support really does make a difference and I read all the reviews personally so I can get your feedback and make this book even better.

Thanks again for your support!

References

Browne, D. (2018, August 31). *How to Let Go: 12 Tips for Letting Go of the Past.* Healthline. **https://www.healthline.com/health/how-to-let-go#1**

Dean, F. (2013, June 5). *How to have more patience.* Chatelaine.

https://www.chatelaine.com/health/sex-and-relationships/how-to-have-more-patience/

Fensterheim, S. (n.d.) *Relationship Advice: Why is Trust so Important?* The Relationship Expert. **https://www.thecouplesexpertscottsdale.co m/2017/08/relationship-advice-trust-important/**

Gans, S. (2019, November 19). *Ways to Rebuild Trust in Your Marriage.* Verywell Mind. **https://www.verywellmind.com/rebuild-trust-in-your-marriage-2300999**

Gaspard, T. (2016, December 7). *10 Ways to Rekindle the Passion in Your Marriage.* The Gottman Institute. **https://www.gottman.com/blog/10-ways-rekindle-passion-marriage/**

Herrin, T. (2020, March 16). *How to Recognize Emotional Disconnect in Your Relationship and What to Do to Reconnect.* ReGain. **https://www.regain.us/advice/general/ho w-to-recognize-emotional-disconnect-in-your-relationship-and-what-to-do-to-reconnect/**

Ishak, R. (2015, December 10). *Little Ways To Be More Open With Your Partner.* Bustle. **https://www.bustle.com/articles/128557-6-ways-to-be-more-open-with-your-partner**

Lancer, D. (n.d.). *24 Tips for Conflict Resolution in an Intimate Relationship.* Gracepoint Wellness.

https://www.gracepointwellness.org/51-family-relationship-issues/article/56557-24-tips-for-conflict-resolution-in-an-intimate-relationship

Linder, A. (n.d.). *Ideas for How to Add Fun Back Into Your Marriage*. All Pro Dad. https://www.allprodad.com/ideas-for-how-to-add-fun-back-into-your-marriage/

Mirchevski, B. (2019, June 16). *Stop with the Excuses — It's Time to Make a Change*. Medium. https://medium.com/the-logician/stop-with-the-excuses-its-time-to-make-a-change-87990fc6a9d6

Moody. (2018, May 16). *The Five Love Languages Defined*. The 5 Love Languages. https://www.5lovelanguages.com/2018/06/the-five-love-languages-defined/

Morin, A. (2020, April 9) *15 Ways to Rebuild a Broken Relationship*. Lifehack. https://www.lifehack.org/articles/communication/10-tips-make-positive-thinking-easy.html

Smith, K. (2018, July 8). *Does Your Relationship Have Positive or Negative Power Struggles?* PsychCentral. https://psychcentral.com/blog/does-your-relationship-have-positive-or-negative-power-struggles/

StockSnap.io - Beautiful Free Stock Photos (CC0). (n.d.). Retrieved March 2, 2020, from **https://stocksnap.io/**

Pegler, L. (2019, October 7). *How to Remain True to Yourself in a Relationship — The Ascent.* Medium. **https://medium.com/the-ascent/how-to-remain-true-to-yourself-in-a-relationship-c836554ac631**

PowerofPositivity. (2019, December 16). *10 Ways to Keep Negativity Out of Your Relationships: Power of Positivity.* Power of Positivity. **https://www.powerofpositivity.com/10-ways-to-keep-negativity-out-of-your-relationships/**

What is Respect in a Healthy Relationship? (2017, February 3). LoveIsRespect. **https://www.loveisrespect.org/content/respect-in-healthy-relationships/**

Made in United States
North Haven, CT
15 January 2022

14812456R00086